# The Essential Work Experience Handbook

## Second Edition

**Arlene Douglas and Séamus O'Neill**

Gill & Macmillan

*To Jim for his patience and support*

*and*

*To Caroline*

*With thanks to Independent Newspapers*

Gill & Macmillan
Hume Avenue
Park West
Dublin 12
with associated companies throughout the world
www.gillmacmillan.ie

© 2006 Arlene Douglas and Séamus O'Neill

ISBN-13: 978 0 7171 4033 6

Print origination in Ireland by TypeIT, Dublin

*The paper used in this book is made from the wood pulp of managed forests. For every tree felled, at least one is planted, thereby renewing natural resources.*

*A catalogue record is available for this book from the British Library.*

# Table of Contents

# Support Material for
## *Essential Work Experience Handbook, 2nd ed.*

Dynamic and easy to use, online support material for this book:

**provides lecturers with:**
- Sample Portfolios
- Web Links

To access Lecturer support material on our secure site:

1) Go to www.gillmacmillan.ie/lecturers

2) Logon using your username and password. If you don't have a password, register online and we will e-mail your password to you.

**provides students with:**
- Sample portfolios
- Web links

To access Student support material:

1) Go to www.gillmacmillan.ie/student

2) Click on the link for Student Support material

# Preface

## Introduction

Work experience, which has been defined as a 'planned experiential learning activity and is an integral part of an educational process' (NCVA 1998), is a mandatory part of many courses of study. This book is aimed at a variety of learners, especially those compiling a work experience portfolio for the Further Education and Training Awards Council (FETAC).

The chapters in the book are designed to guide you through the process of building your work experience portfolio, from planning stage, through the actual work stage and finally to the post-work experience stage, where a review and evaluation of your performance and of the whole experience is carried out.

There is a choice of three modes of undertaking work experience.

1. **Work placement**: The learner gains suitable work experience in an organisation, where the work is monitored by the organisation's manager or supervisor.

2. **Work practice**: The learner undertakes simulated work within their own college or centre's environment, where work is monitored by the tutor.

3. **Work-based learning**: The learner is given Accreditation for Prior Experience, Achievement and Learning (APEAL). Evidence of this must be made available for certification. The learner must also compile a full portfolio of work in line with course requirements (see Chapter 7).

# Chapter outlines

Chapter 1 gives an insight into the nature of work and how it has changed over time.

Chapter 2 provides detailed information regarding what preparations should be made prior to going on work experience, such as how to do a skills audit and how to identify goals for work experience. Sample documents such as a CV and letters of application are included.

Chapter 2 also provides an essential awareness of:

- Interview and job search skills.
- Employment rights and legislation.
- Equality issues.
- Global, technological and demographic trends affecting the workplace.

Chapter 3 explains how a workplace organisational profile can be structured, with sample organisational charts and research questions provided, while on work experience. Information is also available about how to compile a detailed description of actual work undertaken and skills gained during your time on work experience.

Chapter 4 explains how a review and evaluation is carried out after work experience, with questions included to help you with the task of self-reflection regarding your work experience.

Chapter 5 provides guidelines for the workplace supervisor and the learner regarding what to do and what not to do while on work experience. A sample supervisor's form is also included in the chapter.

Chapter 6 provides a guide on how to compile an industry analysis of the workplace job sector. Guidance is also provided regarding the identification of occupations within the sector and their analysis.

Chapter 7 explains to learners with prior suitable work experience how to compile their portfolio for work experience.

Exercises direct the learner to the student workbook that is filled in prior to, during and after work experience. This is intended to be a helpful aid to compiling and completing the work experience portfolio.

# Tips for the learner

Work experience should be an enjoyable, worthwhile exercise helping you, the learner, to gain valuable skills to add to your CV. You are encouraged to include photographs, CDs or audio cassettes, graphic or video evidence to support your written personal accounts of experiences and learning outcomes. The duration of the time spent on work experience is generally a minimum of ten to fifteen days.

## Tip 1: Quality of work

You should aim to learn appropriate skills that are in line with your course of study and choice of career. There is not much point in only being exposed to a narrow range of skills. Do not be afraid to ask for more variety in assigned work tasks and to specify the type of work experience that you would like to be learning.

Consider the following case study as an example.

*Mary, a Business Studies and Computer Applications student, obtained a work placement in AllFiles Travel Ltd. She had hoped to gain useful work experience using a range of software products. One recommended on her chosen vocational course was Galileo (a reservations program used in travel agencies). Instead, every day Mary was given filing duties and had very little opportunity to familiarise herself with the many software products being used by the other employees. Mary mainly worked in a back room and had little interaction with other staff or customers. She was happy to learn the different techniques of filing, photocopying, punching and collating.*

*Looking back, however, Mary said she should have asked the supervisor to allow her to get more involved in the day-to-day working of the business so that she could have gained a greater variety of skills that would have made her more employable.*

## Tip 2: Insurance cover

Make sure appropriate insurance cover is provided for you by your work experience organisation, college or centre.

## Tip 3: What to do when things go wrong

### 1. If you are unhappy in your work placement.

Work experience can sometimes be a source of anxiety and pressure for a learner due to a range of circumstances, e.g. too many duties, insufficient instruction, isolation, difficulty dealing with customers/service users/clients due to lack of experience and colleagues' unwillingness to help.

When things like this happen:

- Consult your class tutor and/or guidance counsellor in the college or centre.
- Approach the supervisor in the workplace and explain the problems.
- Take the initiative and confidently suggest ways in which your learning might be improved upon in the workplace (prepare a written list in advance of speaking to the supervisor/manager).

### 2. If you see or experience something that you consider unacceptable in your workplace, e.g. irregular behaviour or practices.

- Do not discuss the matter openly with other students, friends or staff members in your work placement.
- Bring the matter, in complete confidence, to the attention of the tutor and/or guidance counsellor in the centre or college where you are studying.
- Adopt a professional approach in consultation with your tutor and/or guidance counsellor, and if it is deemed necessary, the matter will be brought to the attention of the appropriate authorities.
- Follow the advice given by the tutor in co-operation with the guidance counsellor in resolving the matter.

### 3. What to do in an emergency.

Ask to be shown where all fire exits and first aid equipment are located, find out who the health and safety representative within the company or organisation is and ask to be briefed on the emergency procedures in the event of an accident. For example, if someone falls on the premises, what is the procedure for dealing with this situation?

In advance of starting work experience, it would be helpful to pick up the Health and Safety Authority leaflet on safety in the workplace and to familiarise yourself with the Safety, Health and Welfare at Work Act (see Chapter 2). Usually, one person in an organisation is in charge of filling out an accident report form that details the date, time, location and nature of an accident, including any witnesses that were present. This person should be trained to deal with emergencies and will be careful not to admit liability in the first instance.

## Tip 4: Special requirements

Check with your workplace to see if there are any special requirements prior to starting on work experience. For example:

- A communications company might require specific training, such as telephone experience.
- An outdoor education centre might require you to be a competent swimmer.
- A crèche or child care establishment may insist that you provide evidence of vaccination against hepatitis or possess a Garda clearance certificate.

## Tip 5: A few words of advice

- Prepare well, take instruction and constructive criticism and adjust your work methods if necessary.
- Keep in mind that the workplace is not your organisation and you don't make the rules!
- Be polite and accommodating to managers, co-workers, customers, suppliers or anyone else you encounter in the workplace.

**Good luck!**

# Sample pre-employment form

| |
|---|
| **WORK EXPERIENCE PRE-EMPLOYMENT FORM** |
| *(To be completed by employers before work experience programme commences)* |

| | |
|---|---|
| Employer name:<br>Address:<br><br><br><br>Telephone:<br>Supervisor name:<br>Position:<br>Department/section:<br>Telephone extension: | Learner name:<br>Address:<br><br><br><br>Telephone:<br>College/centre:<br>Course title:<br>Class:<br>Tutor name: |

| |
|---|
| Job title: |
| Range of duties to be performed by learner on work experience: |
| Range of skills to be acquired by learner on work experience: |
| Signature of tutor/teacher/course provider regarding the suitability of duties/skills listed above:<br><br>Signed: ............................................. Status: ........................ Date: .................... |
| Supervisor/employee signature: ............................................. Date: .................... |

# Chapter One

## The Changing Nature of Work

## What is work?

The *Oxford English Dictionary* describes work as 'an activity involving mental or physical effort done in order to achieve a result or such an activity as a means of earning income.' Work is an essential part of all of our lives. In most cases it provides us with a means of obtaining an income, but it also enables us to develop our talents and reach our potential.

A visit to a local FÁS office or to the careers section in a local library can provide a wealth of information on a wide range of work occupations. A very useful website with thousands of possible career options and corresponding educational and training requirements, work descriptions and salary rates can be found on www.careerdirections.ie.

## CAREER DIRECTIONS

A text based version (WAI Compliant) is available here

UNSURE WHAT CAREER
MIGHT SUIT YOU?

NEED MORE INFORMATION
ON A PARTICULAR CAREER?

NEED HELP TO PLAN YOUR
CAREER WITH CONFIDENCE?

 Start Career Directions

 Jobs Ireland View Current Vacancies and courses on FÁS site
WHERE JOB HUNTERS GO

N.B. You must be running Internet Explorer 5 or higher
with Java Support installed to access this site

## What is work experience?

Work experience is the experience that a person has in the world of work, or of working in a specific field or occupation. We need a job to get experience and experience to get a job.

The term 'work experience' is often used to mean a type of volunteer work that is commonly intended for young people, often students, to get a feel for professional working environments. The work experience placement is mostly unpaid, and at the end of the period, a character reference is usually provided.

**THE WORK CYCLE**

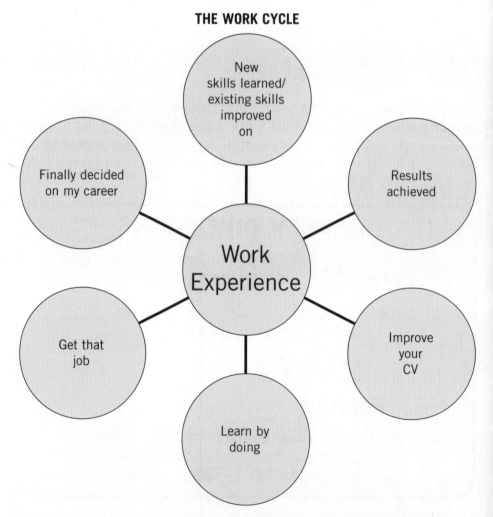

# The three modes of work experience

## Work placement mode

The learner works in an established company or organisation that the course providers have deemed suitable to provide quality work experience. The learner participates in work related to the vocational award area. For example, a student hoping to achieve the FETAC Childcare award may find suitable work experience in a crèche.

## Work practice mode

The learner is involved in a realistic work programme set up by course providers that gives substantial hands-on experience of the vocational area. The work practice must be carefully planned, structured and monitored by course providers. For example, a student wishing to be awarded the FETAC Media Production or Multimedia Production award may be involved in producing a promotional DVD for his or her college.

## Work-based learning mode

This mode is designed to enable learners to gain FETAC accreditation for current or prior experience of work in a vocational area directly related to the certificate being sought. The experience of work must be substantial, verifiable and relevant to the vocational certificate area. For example, this mode is suitable for a learner who has worked for three years as a sales assistant in a busy city centre electrical shop and is now undertaking a course of study leading to the FETAC certificate in Retail Studies.

# Finding a work placement

Looking for a work placement can be a daunting task for many people. The following information may be helpful in finding a suitable placement:

- Think about the type of business or organisation you might like to work in and then find out if there are any in your area.
- A good starting point in looking for work experience is to ask people you know, e.g. family members or friends, to help you find a placement.
- Looking at company advertisements, either in the local paper or in the Golden Pages, can be a big help in finding a business that may offer to take you on a work experience placement.
- Write a letter or e-mail to the owner or managing director, setting out your request for a placement and why you need work experience. Indicate why you are interested in spending some time in the company and what you might be able to do for them.
- Follow up your letter with a telephone call or, better still, a personal visit if you have not had a response within a week.
- Once offered a placement, make sure that it is clearly stated what you are expected to do, the hours you will work and who you will report to.
- At the end of the placement period, think about what you have learned from the experience so that you can articulate your achievements.

## The nature of work in Ireland today

During the 1980s, Ireland's economy performed very poorly. There was no minimum wage and emigration was running at between 40,000 and 50,000 people per year. We were heavily dependent on agriculture and small labour-intensive indigenous industries.

Thankfully, the nature of work in Ireland has seen immense change in recent decades. The economic boom, or 'Celtic Tiger', means people have more money to spend, resulting in the emergence of large retail centres providing greater variety of choice for shoppers. Greater numbers employed and higher wage levels have been the norm since about 1996. There is a movement away from labour-intensive towards capital-intensive industries. Ireland is no longer regarded as a country with a largely agricultural-based economy. In recent years, we have seen the emergence of vibrant electronics, IT and pharmaceutical industries. The change to the euro has also made it easier to compare standards and costs of living in European countries.

Tourism has undergone a huge transformation and is now one of Ireland's biggest areas of employment, helped by the significant decrease in the cost of air travel and the improving road and rail infrastructures within Ireland.

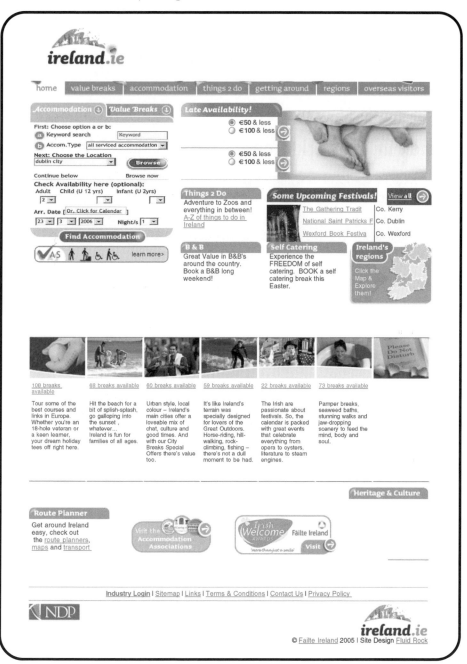

The foundation of the International Financial Services Centre (IFSC) in the 1990s helped to launch Ireland as a leading global player in banking and finance. Service industries such as beauty care and child care are on the increase due to increased wealth and more women in the Irish workforce.

The National Minimum Wage Act provided that from 1 May 2005 the minimum wage rate for an experienced adult employee would be €7.65 per hour.

# Women in the workforce

It is difficult to comprehend that less than forty years ago married women were prevented from working in many occupations. Thankfully, legislation was changed and now women are making an immense contribution to our growing economy. Professions previously considered the preserve of men are now attracting women.

The numbers of women working as architects, company directors, engineers and scientists have increased significantly in recent years, as well as the number of women now holding public office. For the first time, we have a female Minister for Agriculture and the last two Presidents of Ireland have been women.

# The changing nature of work

The clear white-collar, blue-collar distinction that was evident in the 1970s and 1980s no longer exists. In fact, the comfortable permanent pensionable state job is not as attractive to job applicants as it used to be, resulting in skills shortages in areas like primary school teaching.

Significant changes to the time spent in the workplace and the ways that work is carried out are apparent. The traditional 9.00 a.m. to 5.00 p.m. Monday-to-Friday working week is losing its appeal, with many workers now opting for flexi-time and job sharing.

Many workers are also now choosing to telework, i.e. working from home for a number of days each week. Using modern telecommunications, employees can work from home. For example, an employee might work one day per week at her company's Dublin office and on the other four days telework from home in Nenagh, Co. Tipperary.

The advent of the internet and mobile telecommunications means that information can be moved instantaneously and decisions made quickly. Business no longer has to be conducted in the traditional office setting and greater scope now exists for networking for business. Technology such as video conferencing, e-mail and mobile phone text messaging has provided greater worldwide communication, leading to greater product and customer knowledge as well as business competitiveness.

E-business (electronic business conducted via the internet), e-commerce (buying and selling goods and services over the internet) and e-commerce (web advertising) have become accepted as the norm when it comes to twenty-first-century work practices. Online bookings for holidays and online shopping with credit card payment are now the norm. Employees now need IT skills to secure jobs in Ireland's competitive work environment.

## Key national employment trends

**Permanent full-time employment** in manufacturing, internationally traded and financial services and other activities supported by the development agencies rose to 290,600 in 1999, the highest level recorded.

The number of permanent full-time jobs created in 1999 amounted to 34,609, which represents an increase of 7.6 per cent on the levels achieved in 1998 and is the highest to date. However, the level of permanent full-time jobs lost also rose to an all-time high of 21,618 in 1999, an increase of 22.2 per cent on the losses sustained in 1998. This reduced the number of net jobs created in 1999 to 12,991, which is below the levels achieved in 1998 (14,485) and 1997 (15,851).

The key driver of employment growth was internationally traded/financial services activities, which accounted for 9,518 (73.3 per cent) of the total increase of 12,991 in permanent full-time employment in 1999. Permanent full-time employment in manufacturing accounted for 3,480 net jobs, or 26.8 per cent of the total increase in permanent full-time employment recorded in 1999.

**Foreign-owned companies** accounted for 8,713 (67.1 per cent) of net employment growth, with Irish-owned firms contributing the balance of 4,278 (32.9 per cent) net jobs in 1999. Employment grew by 6.3 per cent in foreign-owned firms in 1999 and by 3.1 per cent in Irish-owned companies. This represents a slowdown in the rates of growth achieved by both Irish and foreign-owned firms in recent years.

**On a sectoral basis,** two sectors, internationally traded services and metals and engineering (which includes electronics), accounted for 90 per cent of the net change in permanent full-time employment of 12,991 in 1999. Another sector to perform exceptionally well was international financial services (IFSC-approved companies), which recorded a positive net change in permanent full-time employment of 1,831 (+37.7 per cent) in 1999.

The share of total employment accounted for by part-time, temporary and short-term contract employment in IDA Ireland, Enterprise Ireland and Údarás na Gaeltachta client companies has also increased steadily during the 1990s, rising from 6.7 per cent of all jobs in 1990 to 11 per cent in 1999. This form of employment increased at a faster rate in Irish-owned companies in 1999, rising by 8.1 per cent, compared with a rise of 0.9 per cent in foreign-owned firms.

**On a regional basis,** each region, with the exception of the Border and Midlands regions, recorded a positive net change in permanent full-time employment in 1999. However, the Dublin region fared best, given that it accounted for 31.5 per cent of permanent full-time employment in 1999, but accounted for 63.6 per cent of all net new jobs created in that year. The share of new jobs created in the Border Midlands West (BMW) regions declined in 1998 and 1999, while it increased in the Southern and Eastern regions in these years. It is an aim of industrial policy to achieve a greater regional dispersal in new jobs created. Accordingly, the regional distribution of agency-supported new jobs will be monitored closely in the future.

Permanent full-time employment in manufacturing rose by 18 per cent since 1990, compared with significant falls in a number of other leading industrialised nations. This points to the success of Ireland's policy of developing the manufacturing industry base, which is increasingly focused on high-technology sectors.

People working in the media, e.g. news reporters and correspondents, now transmit news and information from distant countries using e-mail via laptop computers and videophones, thanks to WAP technology. (WAP means wireless application protocol and enables internet access on mobile phones.) News can be received on location at the click of a button.

Communications giants like O$_2$, Meteor and Vodafone have emerged and there is a greater demand for workers in the communications industry as a result.

The Celtic Tiger has ensured that greater employment is available in the housing sector. The National Lotto and Euro Lotto has also meant that the investor is a force to be dealt with and that the property developer could be regarded as a new twenty-first-century career option for risky entrepreneurial types.

The working landscape has also changed, with young people having greater choices of careers. They are increasingly selective when it comes to applying for certain jobs. The enlargement of the EU has meant that a rising number of immigrants are filling job vacancies that Irish workers choose not to apply for. For example, shortages in the hotel and catering sectors have had to be addressed in this way.

# Types of employment

The old traditional sectors of employment used to be referred to as primary, secondary, tertiary and other. Nowadays different definitions exist:

- **Self-employed**: A couple of decades ago, the majority of self-employed people in Ireland tended to be farmers. This has changed in recent years. The number of people in Ireland who have started their own business in areas as diverse as acupuncture and web design has increased greatly. This path to employment is not for everyone and requires a good deal of vision, organisation and dedication. A successful self-employed person can feel a great deal of self-fulfilment and can achieve a good measure of financial reward.
- **Pensionable secure employment**: Public service workers fall into this category, e.g. Gardaí, nurses, teachers.

- **Contract employment**: An individual may be contracted to a company for a six- or twelve-month period to undertake a body of work. Some IT professionals prefer this approach to work.

- **Part-time employment**: An increasing number of part-time workers are joining the workforce. Examples of people in this category are students, semi-retired people or parents with young children.

- **Voluntary employment**: Many people give their free time to work for non-monetary gain. Examples of people in this category are youth club organisers, charity shop sales assistants and hospital radio broadcasters.

# The labour market

The labour market is an important and active area of research at the ESRI and covers a wide range of themes:

## *Labour market dynamics*

Sociologists and economists at the ESRI have been, and are presently involved in, important micro-economic studies of unemployment and labour market dynamics, including:

- the 'employability' of the unemployed
- transitions from school to work
- transitions from unemployment to employment
- transitions from home to work
- the labour market impact of education and training
- the labour market impact of active labour market programmes
- the labour market impact of initial education
- the effects of training at work on both individuals and corporate performance

## *Equality and the labour market*

The ESRI has undertaken a number of important research projects relating to issues of gender and the labour market. These include studies of the male-female wage gap, occupational segregation, women returners, work-life balance and the relationship between fertility and female labour market participation. Gender is also a central concern in research conducted on part-time employment and flexible working.

Equality issues have also been addressed in studies of older workers and will be developed in current work on labour market participation among those with disabilities.

## *Vacancies and skills*

During the recent employment boom, shortages of labour emerged as an important labour market issue. The incidence of vacancies in the private non-agricultural sector of the economy has been investigated in a number of national surveys carried out by the ESRI Survey Unit on behalf of FÁS and Forfás.

The importance for the economy of an adequate supply of skills led to the establishment by the government in 1997 of the Expert Group on Future Skills Needs. Research undertaken for the Expert Group has focused on issues relating to general skill shortages, graduate trends and medium-term demand/supply projections for professionals and technicians in engineering, computer science and other sciences.

## *Occupational forecasting*

The information provided by the FÁS/ESRI series is of considerable value in determining medium-term strategies and in planning training provision. It is necessary to examine trends and developments in the labour market in order to ensure a proper balance of skills as Ireland's economy continues to expand and structural changes occur in the sectoral and occupational composition of employment. For some years, the Institute has been heavily involved in providing medium-term forecasts of the economy. The FÁS/ESRI series provides forecasts in the manpower area which specifically identify the implications of medium-term output and sectoral employment forecasts for the economy's occupational requirements and the educational attainment required to fill the jobs which are likely to be offered by employers in the future.

## *Working conditions*

- Minimum wage.
- Flexible working, including part-time and temporary work.

Research has been carried out for a range of Irish government departments, FÁS and Forfás, the European Commission, the OECD and the ILO. Researchers working in this area participate in a number of European research networks and regularly publish the results of their work in academic journals as well as books and monographs.

*Source:* Economic and Social Research Institute (ESRI) (www.esri.ie).

# Self-evaluation and career choices

Before you embark on a particular career, a good starting point is to make an honest appraisal of your aptitudes, strengths, weaknesses, abilities, aspirations and qualifications.

This is often a difficult but quite revealing and helpful process. If you dislike working in the evenings, then perhaps a career as a chef would not be a wise choice. If you work best by yourself, then a career in hotel management would not suit. If you enjoy numerical analysis and business calculations, then a career in accountancy could be for you.

In doing a self-evaluation and an analysis of a future career, you should look at:

- Aspirations for the future.
- Experiences.
- Future options.
- Abilities and qualifications.

The range of career choices and work options in Ireland has never been better. Some examples of areas of work and corresponding work options are:

- **Agriculture**: Farmer, veterinary surgeon, crop contractor.
- **Media**: Reporters, correspondents, journalists, event managers, film producers, directors.
- **Building**: Carpenter, electrician, plumber.
- **Business**: Accountant, bank official, economist.
- **Catering**: Chef, waiter, health and safety officer.
- **Child care**: Crèche supervisor, nanny, paediatrician.
- **Information technology (IT)**: Network technician, programmer, website designer.
- **Law**: Barrister, legal secretary, solicitor.
- **Public service**: Garda, teacher, political representative.
- **Retail**: Buyer, sales assistant, window display designer.
- **Tourism**: Coach driver, hotel manager, tour operator.

## STUDENT WORKBOOK QUESTIONS

### Exercise 1: Personal introduction
### Now go to your student workbook at the back of this book.

1. On p. 111, write an introduction to your student workbook by introducing yourself. Give a very brief description of your course, subjects being studied, proposed work experience details and any other personal details.

2. Explain what you know about work and work experience in the twenty-first century and your future career plans, i.e. what you want to do and how you plan to get there.

3. Display a critical awareness of how the nature of work and work practices have changed in recent years.

4. Explain how necessary you think it is to obtain work experience.

# Chapter 2

## Learner Record Part 1: Planning and Preparation for Work Experience

It is in your best interests to plan appropriately before going on work experience. We will now examine the best approach to planning and preparation and how to document the details using suitable headings.

## Personal and workplace details

- Name.
- Award title and code.
- Course title.
- Course definition – a brief summary of the nature of the course.
- Subjects being studied.
- Proposed career path.
- Desired location of future work.
- Work experience day(s).
- Proposed times allocated to work experience.

## Skills audit

A skills audit involves identifying the skills that you have learned already and where you learned them. You may have acquired many of these skills at home, in school or through previous work situations. These should be easily identified.

# Personal skills

Personal skills are 'individual skills' and are linked to personality traits, e.g. the ability to work on one's own initiative, meet deadlines, complete tasks successfully, be punctual, speak clearly and be able to work under pressure.

## TABLE 2.1

| Personal skills | Examples |
| --- | --- |
| I'm punctual and have a good attendance record. | I worked in industry for three years and was never late for work. I have very few sick days on record. |
| I'm reliable and able to work on my own initiative. | When employed I was able to take instruction and work on my own – I can supply references to prove it. |
| I'm adaptable/flexible. | Even though I only worked part time, when I worked for a company and retraining was required, I was willing to retrain in order to become computer literate and adapted very well to the new work practices. |
| I'm efficient, committed, good at completing tasks efficiently and meeting deadlines. | When we were organising the school graduation I was allocated the task of jointly producing a graduation booklet. We produced this to meet a set deadline for the printers. |
| I'm a confident person and will dress in a smart, appropriate fashion/be conscious of company image. | I have worked part time as an office administrator and in sales and always dress smartly, usually with a sharp white shirt (and tie) and suit when appropriate, with minimal jewellery and make-up, paying attention to hygiene at all times. This helped me with self-confidence. I've been taught that where customers are concerned, first impressions are lasting. |
| I'm trustworthy, patient and even-tempered. | My previous workplace will verify that I handled complaints and awkward customers very well and remained patient at all times. |

| | |
|---|---|
| I'm good-humoured and have a positive, proactive approach to my work. | My school and my previous workplace will verify that I get on well with classmates, teachers, colleagues and managers and like to move along with my work instead of wasting time. I like to make suggestions for improvement to the workplace when it is appropriate to do so. I also have a good social life. |
| I'm discrete, respectful and reliable. | I was babysitting for a couple for a significant time and respected their privacy at all times. |
| I'm aware of when and when not to articulate my opinion. | I like to make suggestions for improvement to the workplace when it is appropriate to do so and realise that it is not always appropriate to voice your opinion. |
| I'm conscious of maintaining confidentiality and proper company ethics. | I have never discussed information of a personal nature with colleagues or managers to prevent rumours, which are unprofessional and bad for workplace relations and reputation. |
| I'm able to take responsibility and have leadership skills. | I like to take the lead when it comes to organising and making decisions. I captained my local football team, as the manager will verify. |
| I'm a good organiser. | I compiled rosters for my local youth club. |

# Interpersonal skills

Interpersonal skills can be broadly defined as 'people skills', e.g. the ability to deal effectively and efficiently with people and work as part of a team. These skills are displayed when a learner has efficient communication skills.

**TABLE 2.2**

| Interpersonal skills | Examples |
|---|---|
| I communicate well with *employers/ managers* and respect authority. | I have had successful dealings with former teachers and with the manager of the local hurling club that I play for. |
| I communicate well with *colleagues and work partners.* | While in school I was part of a team that organised various Sixth Year events, including our graduation night. |
| I enjoy working with *customers/ clients.* | I work part time in the local corner shop. |
| I enjoy contacting and transacting with *suppliers.* | I worked for my father, who owns a glass shop display business. He set me the task of pricing materials for use in his business. |
| I have experience dealing with *staff who work in personnel and human resources.* | I worked in a HR office for the summer and helped to design a number of advertisements for job vacancies that existed. I had to agree with the manager and change a number of details until we got the ad right. |
| I have experience in negotiating. | I worked for a students' union and dealt with grievances and problems that some students had to the best of my ability. |
| I have good speaking skills/ telephone techniques. | I worked as an office administrator and answered the phone efficiently and courteously. |
| I am aware of my body language when dealing with customers and always try to be confident and helpful. | I had to deal with awkward and rude customers and I did this in a calm and reassuring way, always prioritising the customer. |
| I will always follow up and give appropriate feedback when dealing with customers. | In my capacity as office administrator, I had to call customers back when a consignment of goods that they had ordered arrived. Also, good customer service skills were needed to deal with a number of complaints and I followed up by phoning the customers and apologising for any inconvenience. |

## *Dealing with customers*

When dealing with customers, there are two types of professional interaction:

- face-to-face
- over the telephone.


The following questions will help you identify what kind of face-to-face interpersonal skills you possess:

- Are you good with people?
- Do you have a likeable personality?
- Are you a good listener?
- Are you respectful?
- Are you tactful?
- Are you obliging?
- Do you always put the customer first?
- If possible, would you offer the customer a cup of tea or coffee while they are waiting to see a manager?
- Is it true that you never argue with a customer and you always apologise for any inconvenience, even if you know that the customer was at fault?
- How do you answer the phone in a work situation?
- Have you adopted a professional telephone manner?
- Do you use the correct greeting based on the time of day?
- Do you state your name and offer your assistance?
- If you have to put the caller on hold, do you ask if they mind holding and wait for their answer?

### Role play

*Telephonist:* Good afternoon, Smyth and Cox Brothers Limited. My name is Mary, how may I help you?

*Caller:* I wish to speak to John Smyth, please.

*Telephonist:* Certainly, sir. Can I say who is calling please?

*Caller:* My name is James Turner.

*Telephonist:* Thank you, Mr Turner. Would you mind if I put you on hold for a moment while I see if Mr Smyth is in his office?

*Caller:* That's fine, thank you.

*Telephonist:* All right. Just hold for a moment, thank you.

- Do you always check with your superior or colleague to see if he or she is free to take the call?
- Do you always adopt a professional approach and obtain the caller's name before you put the call through to a superior or colleague?
- Do you always quickly return to the caller and never leave them on hold for longer than a few seconds?
- Do you always take the caller's name and telephone number if necessary and ask if they wish for you to note what the call was regarding?
- Do you always get the message immediately to the person that it is intended to go to?

## Dealing with work colleagues/partners

Along with the qualities outlined above, the following are desirable when dealing with work colleagues:

- Be a good communicator (speaking and listening).
- Work effectively and efficiently as part of a team.
- Be supportive of colleagues.
- Are you even-tempered?
- Do you always make an effort to get on well with work colleagues generally?
- Would you oblige a colleague by covering work hours when it is unavoidable for him/her to work?

## *Dealing with suppliers*

When dealing with suppliers, it is important to realise that there are two different types of purchase:

- Cash purchase, i.e. cash paid over the counter.
- Credit purchase, i.e. purchases on account where it has been agreed that the business has thirty or sixty days' credit. In other words, the business does not have to pay the bill until a month or two after it is received.

When ordering from suppliers, it is important to take the initiative and shop around to get the best value for money.

If you have dealings with suppliers while on work experience, be sure to:

- Check what the business supplies.
- Know what is being ordered and get written confirmation of the order, as well as the time, date and nature of order. (Most businesses have their own order forms that can be faxed to the supplier.)
- Be firm but courteous with suppliers and always check with your supervisor if you are unsure of anything.
- Have you priced around to get the best value for money?
- Do you know what this supplier supplies and how long the business has been ordering goods or services?
- Do you know the terms of trade and if any discounts are allowed? (Usually found on quotations received.)
- Did you check with your supervisor before you phoned the supplier to clarify details?

## *Dealing with the employer/manager*

When dealing with managers, an employee must be able to:

- Portray a bright, cheery and positive image.
- Be trustworthy.
- Be confident regarding your abilities.

- Work on your own initiative.
- Be adaptable.
- Be flexible regarding work hours.
- Be committed.
- Carry out instructions efficiently.
- Accept constructive criticism about your appearance, punctuality and general work conduct.
- Report back to management effectively and efficiently.
- Are you even-tempered?
- Is it true that you never criticise your employer/superior unless it is constructive criticism and is non-confrontational?
- Are you able to accept constructive criticism of your work, appearance, personality and punctuality?
- Will you act on suggestions for personal improvements?

### Dealing with HR/personnel departments

If you are required to deal with a HR head office, make sure you do the following:

- Check with your supervisor if you are dealing with personal details connected with a staff member.
- Know what staff you are enquiring about and their exact status.
- Brief yourself on who exactly you are to speak with in the HR department.
- Always maintain confidentiality when handling personal information – be aware of the Data Protection Act and the rights of employees as well as employer obligations (discussed later in this chapter).

# Practical skills

Practical skills can be defined as 'doing skills', e.g. the ability to perform tasks.

## TABLE 2.3

| Practical skills | Examples |
|---|---|
| Design a company leaflet using Microsoft Publisher. | I have references from the print company that I worked for and samples of my work in the form of a portfolio. |
| Design interiors, having studied on a one-year interior design course. | I have a Certificate in Interior Design and worked part time for a home interiors designer. Written and verbal references are available. |
| I can compile and use spreadsheets. | I have a certificate to show competence in Microsoft Excel. |
| I can use modern sewing machines and make clothes and curtains. | I worked in a curtain shop part time for over two years and have references and work samples available. |
| I have very good writing skills and have some radio broadcasting skills. | I had articles published in a number of different media publications (samples available) and worked part time for a local radio station. |
| I was a plumber and served my time, having done a three-year apprenticeship. | I have a reference from FÁS and the trade certificate. |

Some examples of practical skills that can be learned in different vocational areas are outlined in the following table.

## TABLE 2.4

| Computers and business | Produce a letter on a word processor. Set up a working database of clients. Design a company leaflet using DTP software. Calculate wages, VAT, etc. Produce a cash flow analysis on a spreadsheet. |
|---|---|
| Beauty care | Aromatherapy. Electrolysis. Eyebrow shaping and trimming. Facials. Make-up. Reflexology. Waxing. |

| | |
|---|---|
| **Art and design** | Design solutions from a given design brief.<br>Use pre-press and press techniques.<br>Geometrical constructions.<br>Use colour separation techniques. |
| **Floristry** | Cutting.<br>Arrange dried flowers.<br>Make hand-tied bouquets.<br>Advise customers when taking orders.<br>Watering and tidying plants.<br>Make buttonholes.<br>Greening a wreath. |
| **Retail** | Advertising.<br>Cash and stock control.<br>Computerised space planning.<br>Costing.<br>Pricing.<br>Receiving orders and estimating margins.<br>Signage.<br>Visual merchandising shop display. |

# Technical skills

Technical skills can be described as 'technology skills', e.g. the ability to use and adapt to new technology in an organisation.

**TABLE 2.5**

| Technical skills | Examples |
|---|---|
| I can type. | I have a certificate for basic typing skills that I gained while in school. |
| I can word process a document. | I have already completed the ECDL (European Computer Driving Licence). |
| I can operate a digital telephone switchboard. | I worked for a company as a part-time telephonist – referees will verify. |
| I worked as part of the cabin crew for an airline and learned how to operate the onboard communication system for customer service and safety. | I have appropriate work and character references, who can be contacted immediately. |

# The importance of interests and hobbies

Employers will judge job applicants on qualifications, experience and skills. However, very often a person's skills will be easy to identify through their interests and hobbies.

## TABLE 2.6

| Interest/hobby | What it shows |
|---|---|
| I captained my local hurling team. | Leadership skills. |
| I love animals. I do pony trekking twice a week and clean the animals. | Hard worker and a caring person. |
| I enjoy playing piano and guitar in my spare time. | Musical and creative attributes. |
| I like to make my own clothes. | A stylish and creative person with new ideas. |
| I fly small aircraft and own a few vintage cars. | A risk taker/image conscious. |
| I play football for my home team. | Works well as part of a team. |
| I play kickboxing. | Enjoys a challenge, defensive abilities. |
| I enjoy gardening and learning about new plants and garden design. | Creative and interested in the outdoors. |
| I buy art and invest in stocks and shares. | A creative risk taker with good business acumen. |

## STUDENT WORKBOOK QUESTIONS

### Exercise 2: Skills Audit

**Now go to your student workbook at the back of this book.**

1. Identify your skills using the skills audit worksheet on p. 114. Rate them as indicated.

2. Categorise your skills into personal, interpersonal, practical and technical skills, stating how you hope to learn or improve on these skills and where you originally learned them.

3. Explain how these skills would prove to be an asset to the organisation that you are applying to for work experience.

# Goals for work experience

## *What is a learning goal?*

A learning goal is a target you set or an objective you work towards and aim to achieve. Learners are encouraged to set clear and unambiguous goals for their work experience and document them. This explanation should include the path that leads to achieving the set goals.

Examples of new skills you might hope to achieve while on work experience are to:

- Deal confidently with customers.
- Compile and use a database.
- Produce a word processed document.
- Shoot and edit video footage for a promotional video.
- Design a shop window display.
- Cut and colour hair.
- Gain internet and e-mail skills.

- Expand on good communication skills.
- Learn what personal skills, e.g. negotiating skills, work best in recruitment in a HR department.
- Gain advanced skills used to deal cleverly with different types of people.
- Learn more desktop publishing packages, e.g. Adobe Photoshop and Quark Xpress, in order to work in a print company.
- Improve my typing speed. I have worked with phones, but I have never used a switchboard.

## STUDENT WORKBOOK QUESTIONS

### Exercise 3: Goals for Work Experience

**Now go to your student workbook at the back of this book.**

1. Set and list your goals for this work experience and what skills you hope to learn using the Goals for Work Experience worksheet on p. 118.

# How to compile documents in preparation for work experience

There is nothing worse than badly constructed letters and CVs. When applying for work experience, pay close attention to detail. When compiling documents such as CVs and letters of application, ensure that details are easy to read, with no spelling or grammatical mistakes. Remember: first written impressions are lasting! If you can't do it yourself, pay a professional to do it for you. Don't exclude information that might be critical to a particular employment. It is common for applicants to have slightly different CVs that suit different job positions. For example, when applying for a particular position you might include more details or edit out some details that aren't relevant. The following are guidelines to help you compile a clear, concise CV and letter of application for work experience.

## *The curriculum vitae (CV)*

A CV is a *summary* of your personal details, qualifications, educational details, work experience, skills and interests/hobbies. It should start at the present and work back into the past. It should be no longer than two A4 pages. In order to make it easy to compile, organise a simple table using a word processing computer package, e.g. Microsoft Word, and set up two columns and one row. Insert the headings first in size 12 font, upper case and bold. Subheadings, like dates, should be in sentence case (first word only capitalised). The heading Curriculum Vitae should be outside the table and should be typed first in upper case, bold and centred.

Sample CV headings:

- Personal details.
- Educational details.
- Work experience.
- Skills profile.
- Interests and hobbies.
- Referees.

**TABLE 2.7**

| CURRICULUM VITAE | |
|---|---|
| **PERSONAL DETAILS**<br>Name:<br>Address:<br><br><br><br>Telephone number: | Tom Moore<br>Main Street<br>Westport<br>Co. Mayo<br>085 123 4567 |
| **EDUCATIONAL DETAILS**<br>September 2005–present<br><br><br><br><br>FETAC Certificate<br>Course content<br><br><br><br><br><br>September 1999–June 2005<br><br><br><br><br>(Higher Level)<br><br><br><br>(Lower Level) | Westport Senior College<br>Church Street<br>Westport<br>Co. Mayo<br><br>**Business Studies Administration**<br>Business Administration, Marketing,<br>French, Bookkeeping, Accounting,<br>Statistics, Word Processing, Database,<br>Communications, Work Experience<br><br>Ard Scoil Mhuire<br>Friar Street<br>Westport<br>Co. Mayo<br><br>Leaving Certificate<br>French (C3), Maths (C2), Business (C1),<br>Biology (D1), Physics (D1)<br><br>English (A2), Irish (B2) |
| **WORK EXPERIENCE**<br>September 2006–Present<br><br><br><br><br>March 2005 to August 2006 | **Shop assistant**<br>XtraVision<br>Main Street<br>Westport<br>Co. Mayo<br><br>**Office clerk**<br>Brian and Burrows Solicitors<br>High Street<br>Westport<br>Co. Mayo |

| **SKILLS PROFILE** | |
|---|---|
| Computer literacy | Good working knowledge of Microsoft Word, Excel and Access. Internet and e-mail skills. |
| Personal skills | Good people skills and good timekeeper. Experience with telephone switchboard. |
| Achievements | Full clean driving licence. Grade 8 in Piano Royal Academy of Music. Won various medals in hockey for Ard Scoil Mhuire, Mayo. |
| Interests | I enjoy playing piano, singing and reading. I am a member of Westport Musical Society. |
| **REFEREES** | Ms Jean Black, Course Tutor<br>Westport Senior College<br>Church Street<br>Westport, Co. Mayo<br>Tel: 090 34454<br><br>Mr Roy White, Principal<br>Ard Scoil Mhuire<br>Friar Street<br>Westport, Co. Mayo<br>Tel: 090 55657 |

## *The letter of application for work experience*

Modern-day letter writing consists of a more straight-line layout, with all information left aligned. This layout is clear, concise and easy to read.

- The inside name and address is the name or status of the person you are writing to, e.g. Ms Mary Cotter or The Manager.
- The salutation can either be:
  - 'Dear Sir or Madam', where the complimentary close is 'Yours faithfully' or 'Truly'.
  - 'Dear Ms Cotter', where the complimentary close is 'Yours sincerely'.
- The subject heading is the subject of the letter, e.g. Work Experience Application or Job Application. ('Re:' or 'regarding' is no longer used.)

## Sample letter of application

22 The Crescent
South Circular Road
Limerick

15 October 20XX

Ms Mary Smyth
HR Manager
GE Capital Ltd
Shannon, Co. Clare

Dear Ms Smyth,

**APPLICATION FOR WORK EXPERIENCE**

I wish to apply for work experience with your organisation for the duration of 10 working days, from 6 February 20XX to 17 February 20XX inclusive.

At present I am studying at Limerick Senior College and my chosen course of study is a one-year FETAC Certificate in Marketing with a Language. Work experience is a mandatory module on this course.

I would be very grateful if you could arrange some work experience for me in the areas of sales and marketing or customer service.

Please find enclosed a recent edition of my Curriculum Vitae.

I look forward to hearing from you.

Yours sincerely,

Joan Black
Enc

## *Letter of introduction to the employer*

The employer letter is generally designed and given to the learner during their studies prior to work experience. The course tutor usually issues this introductory letter on behalf of the institution the learner is studying at.

### Sample letter of introduction to the employer

---

**Leitrim College of Further Education**
**Carrigallen**
**Co. Leitrim**
**Telephone: 048 23323   Fax 048 24454**
**Email www.leitrimfe.ie**

7 January 20XX

Mr John White
Insurance Broker
Main Street
Carrigallen
Co. Leitrim

Dear Mr White,

**WORK EXPERIENCE**

Thank you for accommodating our student for a period of work experience from 9 February 20XX to 20 February 20XX.

Work Experience is a requirement for the FETAC Certificate in Business Studies/Administration. As you can appreciate, it is of great benefit to the students to gain useful work experience in financial services and/or insurance.

Some of the subjects studied by the students include e-business, banking/financial services. Also, many of them have opted to sit the professional insurance foundation exam with the Insurance Institute of Ireland (IF1).

The students should also be capable of carrying out routine office duties that include word processing, database, spreadsheet and accounts. The programs that they use in the college are Microsoft Office (Word, Access and Excel) as well as

---

Tas Books. They also study web design, business administration and communications.

The college provides insurance cover for the students during the period of work experience.

If you need to clarify anything with me, feel free to e-mail me any time at jblack@westportsc.ie

Yours sincerely,

_____

Jean Black
Course Tutor

# The insurance letter

### Insurance requirements for work experience

Most employers will look for proof of student insurance before students are accepted for work experience. Most course providers will provide this insurance cover for students with an accompanying letter stating the extent of coverage for any liability incurred. This varies depending on the course provider. It is very important that the student makes sure that they are covered by insurance by either the employer or the course provider or both.

# How to prepare for the interview

You must prepare well for an interview with a prospective employer.

### Workplace background analysis

Find out some information about the company or organisation that you are going to be interviewed by.

- What is the manager's/owner's name?
- What products/services are produced?
- How many people are employed at the organisation?
- How many branches are there, nationally or internationally?

## Job background analysis

Find out what the job requirements are and what will be expected of you. It is favourably looked on if you telephone the manager who will be interviewing you in advance in order to find out this information if it is not otherwise readily available to you.

## CV audit

After the initial greeting, the starting point of every interview is an employer scan of the candidate's CV.

Precisely identify your practical skills and where you learned them, your personal qualities and skills, your interpersonal skills and where you learned them and your unique selling point (USP), i.e. why you are the most suitable person for the job. Then link your skills (practical, personal and interpersonal) with the job you are being interviewed for.

In summary, you must:

- Research the nature of the job you are being interviewed for.
- Examine your skills, abilities and past work experience.
- Try to relate your skills, abilities and work experience to the needs of the job.

## Speech

Anticipate likely questions by consulting with your family and friends. Summarise your answers to these anticipated questions.

A confident delivery that shows evidence of planning is essential. Planning your speech is the key to good organisation. This will minimise any nervousness you may experience in advance of the interview.

## Appearance/dress and body language

Always remember that first impressions at interviews are lasting. It is important to:

- Dress appropriately (formal dress) for the interview.
- Pay attention to tidiness and good personal hygiene.
- Be aware of your body language, e.g. fidgeting, crossing legs, slouching.
- Be aware of the importance of eye contact with the interviewer.

# Interview tips for job hunters

Skills are in high demand and there are plenty of job opportunities. However, bear in mind that employers have increasingly high standards and want to select the best. To prove that you are the best candidate, keep the following in mind.

CVs should be well presented, two pages long, with no spelling mistakes and highlight your skills and experience. Don't worry about getting your CV bound, it makes no difference to what is inside.

Check every avenue for details of job opportunities. Ask friends, relatives, former employers, look in the newspapers and on the Internet, visit the High Skills Pool Jobs Fair.

If you don't hear back from companies, phone them and ask if you can come for an interview.

The standard of job interviews is high. Be honest in what you say and think of factual answers to questions like 'Tell us about yourself' (start with something recent, not your childhood); 'Describe a situation where you have had to deal with stress' (e.g. dealing with an angry person); 'Have you ever had to follow a set of written instructions?' (remember if you have completed an aptitude test as part of the interview process, this is an example); 'Have you ever had to work with someone who let down the team?' (remember, it takes all sorts – give an accurate example if you have had this experience but remember to mention that person's good points too).

If you are asked about dealing with changing circumstances, remember that flexibility at work is considered very important by employers in Ireland, so avoid describing something that 'wasn't in my job description'.

Never criticise a former employer at interview.

You may find yourself being asked the same questions by different interviewers in the same company. You still need to answer fully each time and be consistent. The interviewers will be comparing notes afterwards and consider consistency as a positive.

You need to show the employer that you are interested in them. Find out what you can about the company in advance – most companies will send you information if you contact them.

Prepare a list of questions to ask at interview, for example:

• Why has the vacancy arisen?
• What are your company's/department's goals for the next quarter/year?
• Do you have any plans to expand into new markets?
• What is your most successful product and why?
• What is your company culture – for example, do you work in teams?
• Is training provided? If you have certain skills that you could pass onto others in the company, will you be given that opportunity?
• Do employees meet socially?
• Does the company have links with the community, e.g. sponsoring charities, providing work placements for the unemployed?

And, finally, remember that you may not be offered every job you apply for. However, keep in touch with companies that you do meet, write a thank you letter after interviews even if you are rejected first time, ask for feedback and let them know you're interested in future opportunities. Ireland is very small and you are guaranteed to come across the same people again.

© Independent Newspapers

# Selling yourself

## Getting through the job interview

The three key attributes towards landing that job are appearance, application and attention. There may be thousands of vacancies out there but you still have to undergo that dreaded interview.

Academic qualifications are not enough in the days when the ability to sell oneself to a prospective employer is king. Many human resources managers look for the other qualities in a person besides their basic qualifications when interviewing for a position.

Good appearance and communications skills are imperative. Some interviewers may also ask the applicant to undergo a psychometric test. This consists of a series of questions that can be used to analyse a candidate's ability and personality.

It involves a rapid personality questionnaire where the candidate is asked to answer eighty questions by determining how well particular adjectives apply to them.

A personality profile of the applicant is then compiled under the following five headings: extroversion, confidence, structural, toughmindedness and conformity.

A concise curriculum vitae is essential. It shouldn't be more than two A4 pages and it should list your work history, education record, achievements as well as personal details such as leisure and sports interests. But remember, the employer doesn't have the time or inclination to wade through pages and pages of your background.

Research the company you are hoping to work for. Familiarise yourself with as much background as you can and have a few questions ready to ask about the company during your interview.

During the interview be positive, show you are flexible and try to be as relaxed as possible. Rehearse the obvious questions such as 'Why do you want to join us?' and 'Why did you leave your last job?'

Don't be afraid to sell yourself. Companies want people who are not afraid to show that they are dynamic and energetic, says Brendan Devine, recruitment specialist with ETC Consultants. Be confident without being cocky. There used to be a tendency to underestimate personal qualities but that has now changed and companies want people who are enthusiastic and energetic, he says.

Avoid extremes of dress or strong perfume as they could result in instant poor impression. Don't be taken in by a relaxed, easy-going manner.

Don't slouch in the chair or fidget. Be positive even if tricky or aggressive questions are thrown at you.

If asked about your previous job do not criticise your former or current employers as this can indicate a lack of loyalty which will count against you.

Finally, don't wait for the employer to get back to you with an answer. Apply for other jobs in the meantime.

© Independent Newspapers

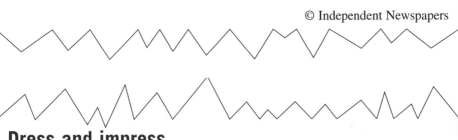

# Dress and impress

## First impressions at interviews are most important

Skilled and unskilled workers are likely to be rubbing shoulders these days in the reception rooms of the country's recruitment agencies.

Factory operatives are now visiting the job placement experts instead of turning up 'on the job' seeking work. And many are now being employed on rollover three-month contracts depending on the job.

Manufacturing companies are sourcing more of their staff from employment agencies as the industry struggles to cope with staff shortages. A factory worker will earn a basic £5 to £6 an hour plus perks in Dublin.

'There is a huge demand for people across the board. There has been a thirty to forty per cent increase in vacancies in all areas of industry,' said Adrian McGennis, of recruitment specialists, the Marlborough Group. All IT positions are in demand plus engineering technicians, accountants and senior sales professionals.

But he said many companies have now changed their recruitment policies. The days of turning up for a one-on-one interview are over. The candidate is likely to undergo a psychometric test, role play and functional examinations in addition to a forty-five-minute interview.

'We would advise candidates to prepare well for their interview, find out as much as possible about the company and have a number of questions prepared,' said Mr McGennis.

Lack of preparation is one of the biggest criticisms of people going for interviews. 'Some people can appear too arrogant and others reply to questions with a "yes" or "no" instead of expanding on their answer.'

If a candidate is unsure about a dress code for an interview, be conservative and wear a suit and tie. It is better to be over-dressed. Be yourself, make eye contact and have positive thoughts.

© Independent Newspapers

## Job search skills

A job description consists of the job title, location, duties and any other special features relevant to the post being advertised.

A job specification refers to the special qualities, qualifications and skills that are sought by an organisation. These usually do not appear in a newspaper advertisement. Candidates are encouraged to phone, check a company website or write to the organisation concerned for these details.

*Child care advertisement*

# ATHLONE COMMUNITY TASKFORCE

**ACT is a community group established in 1992 to implement
local economy and social development initiatives for the
Athlone Urban Area.
We are now seeking to fill the position of:**

# CHILDCARE DEVELOPMENT WORKER

The successful candidate will assist with the identification, development and implementation of a Community Childcare Strategy for Athlone. The ideal candidate should have a recognised qualification in a Childcare-related area and have at least 3 years experience in Childcare and Community Activities. He/she will have the capacity to devise and implement an integrated cohesive, comprehensive and multi-sectoral approach to Childcare Development in Athlone. He/she will have the skills to interact effectively and to foster co-operation and consensus with a broad range of individuals and groups which includes excellent skills in networking, facilitation, evaluating, administration and capacity building. The position which is funded under the ADM Equal Opportunities Childcare Programme is on a contract basis. Applicants should send their CV before closing date of 1st September to: (mark envelope CDW)

**JIMMY KEANE C.E.O.**
**Athlone Community Taskforce, Parnell Square, Athlone, Co. Westmeath**

## Tourism sales manager advertisement

# Customer Sales Manager

As part of the Holidaybreak PLC Group, Keycamp Holidays is Ireland's leading self-drive camping and mobile home tour operator. We take pride in delivering the very highest level of service and due to an expanding product range, which includes camping holidays and UK hotel breaks as part of our Superbreak brand, we are seeking to appoint an experienced professional to become part of our highly successful team based in Cork.

The Customer Sales Manager would be responsible for a team of twelve people, and with a minimum of five years' management experience, you will play a key role in the business and sales strategy, setting team and individual targets. Your role will include conducting competitor surveys and comparisons, the training and recruitment of new staff along with the coaching and monitoring of sales calls to evaluate staff performance and identify training needs.

Educated to degree level, you should possess the ability to deliver a professional client-focused service at all times. With a confident personality and excellent communication skills, you should enjoy dealing with clients at all levels and possess the ability to be able to work on your own initiative or as part of a team, with flexibility towards daily duties and working hours. Travel industry/self-drive camping market experience and knowledge of customer relations or public relations are highly desired.

Applications, IN WRITING ONLY, enclosing a full CV with covering letter stating why you wish to work for Keycamp Holidays to:

### The Human Resources Manager
### Keycamp Holidays
### 78–80 South Mall, Cork

### Closing date: I September

In the search for a job and/or work experience, many methods are used:

- Direct application to employer, combined with a follow-up phone call. No advertisement in paper.
- Application in response to a newspaper advertisement (perhaps seen on a noticeboard or referred to by a friend or career guidance counsellor) or job finder catalogue advertisement.
- Use of recruitment agencies, which can be found on the internet, in the Golden Pages, in job finder catalogues, on noticeboards, etc.
- Make an appointment to meet the personnel officer or manager of an organisation you are interested in working for.
- Networking, i.e. using friends or family connections in the effort to secure a job.

**Word of advice:** Don't wait until you have finished your course to apply for jobs. While you are on work experience, you should be actively engaged in searching for jobs, keeping an eye open for suitable positions that match your prospective qualifications.

The following websites may be useful:

- www.corporateskills.com
- www.crc-international.com
- www.exp.ie
- www.hrm.ie
- www.intel.ie
- www.jobfinder.ie
- www.overseasjobs.com
- www.topjobs.ie

Search engines that can be used to browse the internet include:

- www.ask.com
- www.dogpile.com
- www.google.ie

# Contracts of employment

There are two different types of employment contracts:

- **Permanent contract**: An employee is contracted on a permanent basis. This type of employment is usually pensionable, i.e. the employee contributes towards a pension through their wages for their retirement.
- **Temporary contract**: The employer offers a contract to an employee for a set period of time. This contract expires on the date stated. An employer may offer an applicant a renewal period where another contract is drawn up.

A sample contract of employment, sample terms and conditions of employment form and sample declaration of secrecy form can be found at the end of this chapter.

## STUDENT WORKBOOK QUESTIONS

### Exercise 4

**Curriculum vitae, letters, insurance forms, contracts of employment, job-finding skills and interview preparation.**

**Now go to your student workbook at the back of this book.**

1. Create a rough draft of your CV in the space provided on p. 120.
2. Draft a letter of application for work experience on p. 122.
3. In your portfolio of work include any insurance letters, contracts or correspondences that you sent to or received from your prospective employer for work experience.
4. Explain how you plan to gain work experience using your job-finding skills.
5. Give a concise account of your preparations for the interview for work experience. This should include how you plan to dress, sit and speak and a CV analysis using the main question: 'Why am I the best candidate for the position?'

# Health, safety and welfare in the workplace

The Health and Safety Authority (HSA) is a state-sponsored body under the Department of Enterprise, Trade and Employment and has the overall responsibility for the administration and enforcement of health and safety at work in Ireland. It monitors compliance with legislation at the workplace and can take enforcement action, including prosecutions. The health and safety of people at work and of the public affected by work activities is protected by law, namely the Safety, Health and Welfare at Work Act 1989 (explained below). It is an employer's obligation to their employees to ensure a safe work environment without risk to health. Specifics regarding buildings are usually documented in a 'Safety Statement' that must be made available to both health and safety inspectors and employees on request. Workplace bullying is also a health and safety issue that can be challenged under the Safety, Health and Welfare at Work Act 1989.

# Employment equality

This is defined as the right that all workers in the country have to be treated equally and not to be the subject of employment discrimination. The Equality Authority is an independent state body in Ireland set up in 1999 (which replaced the Employment Equality Agency) that can provide information to the public on equality legislation. At its discretion, it can also provide legal assistance to people who wish to bring claims to the Equality Tribunal. The Circuit Court deals with claims about gender discrimination.

There are two main pieces of legislation in place in Ireland that set out important rights for citizens and outlaw discrimination when it occurs: the Employment Equality Act 1998 (amended 2004) and the Equal Status Act 2000 (as amended by the Equality Act 2004). Anyone providing opportunities, services or agencies where the public has access cannot discriminate on nine distinct grounds: gender, marital status, family status, sexual orientation, religion, age (does not apply to a person under sixteen) disability, race and membership of the Traveller community.

## *Equality issues/definitions*

- **Positive action:** In recent years, employers have been encouraged to establish policies and procedures to show that they are taking reasonable steps to demonstrate their commitment to equality and to avoid discrimination in the work environment. Usually these policies and procedures are documented in the form of an Equal Opportunities Policy and grievance procedures (employee complaints procedures) in an employee handbook, usually available from an organisation's human resources department. Employers also promote positive action by organising anti-racism and anti-harassment/anti-bullying training for staff. The aim is to comply with equality legislation and to avoid discrimination.

- An **ethnic group** is defined by a common identity, kinship, ancestry, culture, history or tradition. For example, the Traveller community is Ireland's largest ethnic minority, although in recent years immigration has created a multicultural Ireland. Ethnic groups can sometimes be defined based on having a common religion or language, e.g. Protestants and Catholics in Northern Ireland.

- **Ethnicity** describes the identity with or membership of a particular racial, national or cultural group and observance of that group's customs, beliefs and language. Ethnic groups can exist comfortably as part of a different race, e.g. the Chinese community in New York.

- **Racial and religious equality** means promoting equality among the races and respecting and understanding cultural diversity, religion and customs.

- **Gender equality** means promoting equality between the sexes.

- **Age equality** means promoting equality for people aged over 50.

- **Disability equality** means promoting equality for the disabled.

- **Sexual orientation** means promoting equality for non-heterosexual workers (gays and lesbians as well as transgender).

Equality regarding workplace bullying and sexual harassment:

- **Harassment** is defined as 'unwanted conduct of a sexual nature or other conduct based on sex affecting the dignity of women and men at work.'

- **Bullying** is verbal, physical or psychological aggression engaged in by an employer against employees or by an employee or a group of employees against another employee. It can take the form of intimidation, isolation, victimisation, exclusion, shouting, abusive behaviour, constant criticism or nagging, verbal threats, physical threats, humiliation, excessive controlling behaviour, unreasonable behaviour or task assignment or posters, banners, e-mails and emblems that cause offence.
- **Equality regarding marital and family status** means promoting equality for men, women and children in the home.

## Union representation in the workplace

A union is group of workers that makes representation for common work entitlements regarding pay and conditions in the workplace. There are three main types of union.

- **Craft unions:** The skilled category, e.g. Irish Print Union.
- **White-collar unions:** Professional, office and service occupations, e.g. Teachers Union of Ireland (TUI).
- **General unions:** Semi-skilled and unskilled workers, e.g. Services, Industrial, Professional and Technical Union (SIPTU).

The Irish Congress of Trade Unions (ICTU) is the umbrella organisation for most of the bigger unions of workers in Ireland and represents employees at the Social Partnership talks, i.e. talks between government representatives, employer representatives, e.g. IBEC and SFA, and other interested groups, e.g. Combat Poverty Agency. Pay structures and work conditions are recommended and negotiated and usually a National Wage Agreement is secured for workers, such as Partnership 2000. Public sector workers like nurses and civil servants are promised incremental pay increases.

The **minimum wage** is the minimum a worker can legally be paid (usually per hour), as opposed to wages that are determined by the forces of supply and demand in a free market. In most cases, the minimum wage acts as a price floor. Each country sets its own minimum wage laws and regulations, and many countries have no minimum wage. The current minimum wage is €7.65 per hour in Ireland.

## *Equal opportunities in employment*

Employers are legally obliged to adhere to the existing equality legislation when hiring and employing staff, whether they are full time or part time. When you are an employee or a prospective candidate, your employer cannot discriminate against you, as follows.

- **The recruitment procedure:** Discriminatory manner or questions during the interview (you have a right to information through an equality officer if you suspect discrimination has or is taking place).
- **Access to employment:** Having different entry requirements for you compared to other applicants.
- **Conditions of employment:** Unequal terms of employment and work conditions, overtime, shift work, transfers or dismissals (except remuneration).
- **Training, experience:** Your employer must provide the same opportunities or facilities for employment counselling and training and work experience as those offered to other employees in similar circumstances.
- **Promotion or regrading:** Access to promotional opportunities must be allowed by your employer as is allowed to similarly qualified or other candidates.

Information on Employment Equality Legislation is available on www.equality.ie

# Employee and employer rights and responsibilities

The main duties of the employee are to:

- Be available for work and provide a good service.
- Obey orders from superiors/employers.
- Exercise their work duties with diligence and an acceptable level of efficiency.
- Maintain confidentiality regarding company information.
- Be willing to compensate the employer for any damage caused or wrongful act committed.

The main duties of the employer are to:

- Recognise equality issues and equal opportunities related to the workplace, e.g. gender, age, sexual orientation, ethnicity, race, marital status, etc.
- Insure employees appropriately in the workplace. (Most businesses are covered by full public liability insurance.)
- Adhere to the safety, health and welfare legislation.
- Respect employee representation by their trade unions.
- Pay employees at an appropriate wage level as agreed by the social partners in National Wage Agreements, such as Partnership 2000. The social partners include the government, ICTU, the Irish Business and Employers' Confederation (IBEC), the Irish Tourist Industry Confederation (ITIC), the Small Firms Association (SFA) and others.
- Inform workers of their rights regarding their terms of employment by providing employees with a written statement of these terms.
- Provide workers with appropriate minimum notice before the termination of a contract of employment.

# Current employment legislation in Ireland

The following twelve legal acts outline employee rights and employer obligations.

---

- **Maternity Protection Act 1994:** Provides maternity protection for an employee who works for eight or more hours per week for the one employer or is employed under a fixed-term contract for in excess of twenty-six weeks.
- **Parental Leave Act 1998:** Enables men and women to avail of fourteen weeks of *unpaid leave* to be taken before the child reaches five years of age, or in the case of an adoptive child to be taken within two years of the adoption order; and to provide for limited paid leave to enable employees to deal with family emergencies.

- **Payment of Wages Act 1991:** Entitles every employee to an agreed mode of payment, a written statement of gross wages and deductions and protection against unlawful deductions from wages.

- **Holiday Employee's Act 1973:** Entitles employees to annual leave and holiday pay in a 'leave year' (1 April to 31 March).

- **Worker Protection (Regular Part-time Employees) Act 1991:** Provides that part-time employees working eight or more hours per week who have been in the continuous service of the employer for not less than thirteen weeks (and who are not covered by the Holiday Employee's Act 1973) are to get annual leave at the rate of six hours for every 100 hours worked.

- **Protection of Young Person's (Employment) Act 1997:** Aims to protect young workers under the age of eighteen.

- **Employment Equality Act 1998 (amended to The Equality Act 2004):** Describes discrimination as the treatment of one person in a less favourable way than another person is, has been or would be treated. Discrimination is outlawed on nine distinct grounds: gender, marital status, family status, sexual orientation, religious belief, age, disability, race and membership of the Traveller community.

- **Minimum Notice and Terms of Employment Acts 1973–94:** Entitles employees to information about their terms of employment in writing and the minimum periods of notice to be given by employers and employees when terminating a contract of employment.

- **Unfair Dismissals Acts 1977–93:** Protects employees from being unfairly dismissed and gives redress to those who have been unfairly dismissed.

- **Redundancy Payment Acts 1967–91:** These Acts oblige an employer to pay compensation to employees who are dismissed due to redundancy. A lump sum payment is made to the redundant worker based on age, years of continuous service and gross weekly wage.

- **Safety, Health and Welfare at Work Act 2005:** The Act places responsibility on employers to provide a healthy and safe environment for employees to work in.

- **Data Protection Act 2003:** Protects personal information on private people stored on computers.

- **Freedom of Information Act 2003:** Obliges government departments, Health Service Executive (HSE) crews, local authorities and a range of other statutory agencies to publish information on their activities and to make personal information available to citizens.

Source: www.irlgov.ie.

# Employment law update in Ireland

The following is a summary of the legislation that has been introduced from 1993 to 2004 concerning employment protection.

- **Maternity Protection Amendment Act 2004:** This legislation makes significant improvements to previous maternity protection legislation. From 18 October 2004, new provisions will be introduced relating to ante-natal classes, additional maternity leave, breastfeeding, reduction in compulsory period of pre-birth confinement, etc.

- **Equality Act 2004:** This legislation makes significant amendments to the Employment Equality Act 1998, such as providing for extension of the age provisions of that Act to people under the school leaving age (from sixteen) and those over sixty-five years. It also amends the Equal Status Act 2000 to extend the definition of sexual harassment and shift the burden of proof from the complianant to the respondent.

- **Protection of Employees on Transfer of Undertakings Regulations 2003:** This legislation applies to any transfer of an undertaking, business or part of a business from one employer to another employer as a result of a legal transfer (including the assignment or forfeiture of a lease) or merger. Employees' rights and entitlements are protected during this transfer.

- **Protection of Employees (Fixed Term Work) Act 2003:** This legislation protects fixed-term employees by ensuring that they cannot be treated less favourably than comparable permanent workers and that employers cannot continually renew fixed-term contracts. Under the Act employees can only work on one or more fixed-term contracts for a continuous period of four years. After this the employee is considered to have a contract of indefinite duration', e.g. a permanent contract.

- **Organisation of Working Time (Records) (Prescribed Form and Exemptions) Regulations 2001:** The main purpose of this EU Regulation is the requirement by employers to keep a record of the number of hours worked by employees on a daily and weekly basis, to keep records of leave granted to employees in each week as annual leave or as public holidays and details of the payments in respect of this leave. Employers must also keep weekly records of starting and finishing times of employees.

- **Protection of Employees (Part-Time Work) Act 2001:** This replaces the Worker Protection (Regular Part-Time Employees) Act 1991. It provides for the removal of discrimination against part-time workers where such exists. It aims to improve the quality of part-time work, to facilitate the development of part-time work on a voluntary basis and to contribute to the flexible organisation of working time in a manner that takes account of the needs of employers and workers. It guarantees that part-time workers may not be treated less favourably than full-time workers.

- **Carer's Leave Act 2001:** This provides for an entitlement for employees to avail of temporary unpaid carer's leave to enable them to care personally for persons who require full-time care and attention.

- **National Minimum Wage Act 2000:** Introduces an enforceable national minimum wage.

- **Employment Equality Act 1998:** Prohibits discrimination in a range of employment-related areas. The prohibited grounds of discrimination are gender, marital status, family status, age, race, religious belief, disability, sexual orientation and membership of the Traveller community. The Act also prohibits sexual and other harassment.

- **Parental Leave Act 1998:** Provides for a period of unpaid leave for parents to care for their children and for a limited right to paid leave in circumstances of serious family illness (force majeure).

- **Organisation of Working Time Act 1997:** Regulates a variety of employment conditions including maximum working hours, night work, annual and public holiday leave.

- **Protection of Young Persons (Employment) Act 1996:** Replaced previous legislation dating from 1977 and regulates the employment and working conditions of children and young persons.
- **Adoptive Leave Act 1995:** Provides for leave from employment principally by the adoptive mother and for her right to return to work following such leave.
- **Terms of Employment (Information) Act 1994:** Updated previous legislation relating to the provision by employers to employees of information on such matters as job description, rate of pay and hours of work.
- **Maternity Protection Act 1994:** Replaced previous legislation and covers matters such as maternity leave, the right to return to work after such leave and health/safety during and immediately after the pregnancy.
- **Unfair Dismissals Act 1993:** Updates and amends previous legislation dating from 1977.

## Complaints/breach of rights

Employment law in Ireland provides strong protection for employees who feel their rights have been breached. Complaints, disputes and grievances are heard before a **Rights Commissioner** who will listen to both sides before completing an investigation of the complaint and issuing a recommendation. Recommendations issued by the Rights Commissioner can be binding or non-binding, depending on the type of law under which the case is heard.

Claims under equality legislation are brought to the **Equality Tribunal**.

Often, disputes between employers and employees can be resolved using mediation. Mediation means that the **Labour Relations Commission** is contacted and appoints an independent person to meet with both parties and listen to both sides. This free service is available to all employees and employers (except members of the Gardaí, defence forces and prison services). Meetings are held privately and all discussions are confidential.

## How to apply

Requests for mediation services should be made to the **Director of Conciliation Services at the Labour Relations Commission.**

Complaints, disputes or grievances regarding breaches of employment rights under certain legislation can be heard before a Rights Commissioner. Before you apply to have your complaint heard, you must notify you employer of your intention to contact the Rights Commissioner service. Where legal entitlements are involved, you should try and resolve the matter locally before referring to the Rights Commissioner service.

Source: Oasis (www.oasis.gov.ie).

## STUDENT WORKBOOK QUESTIONS

### Exercise 5: Employment Equality, Health and Safety Legislation

### Now go to your student workbook at the back of this book.

1. In the space provided on p. 127, indicate what you know about employment equality and the two main legal Acts underpinning it.

2. What are an employer's main obligations?

3. Explain how your employer can take positive action to prevent workplace discrimination.

4. List and explain ten pieces of current legislation relating to employment in Ireland.

# Key issues influencing trends in the vocational area

In preparation for work experience, it is important that you recognise how changes in world events, globalisation, technology and population have affected or will have future effects on your chosen area of study and the industry you hope to gain work experience in.

Demographic changes, globalisation and rapid technological change are the three major challenges facing Europe today. You should try to ascertain if your workplace and the industry that it is part of have been affected by these key issues.

## *Demographic shifts*

'Demographics' is a shorthand term for 'population characteristics'. It is the study of human population and its structure and change. It examines how populations are dispersed and how the birth and death rates fluctuate over time, causing changing demographic structures in different countries. The most frequently used demographic variables are age, gender, sexual orientation, family size, household size, family cycle, income, occupation, education, home ownership, socio-economic status, religion and nationality. In addition to demographic variables, a population can be segmented based on psychographic, geographic and behavioural variables.

The most noticeable changes in population (demographic shifts) in Ireland have been due to the following:

- **A fall in the active working population:** A future decline in the active working population is expected and skills shortages are already becoming apparent. There is consequently a need for more working women (promoting gender equality at work) and better child care arrangements. Job sharing has also become the norm to facilitate working women. This option is also open to men.

- **An ageing population:** There will be a continuing need for additional care for the increasing number of elderly, and soaring social security costs are becoming evident as a result. The Carers Allowance has marked the beginning of this demographic shift in Ireland. The promotion of a flexible retirement age is also now desirable.

- **Immigration:** Incoming migrants and refugees residing in different parts of Ireland and have come to Ireland because of war and economic instability in their countries of origin, e.g. Nigeria, the Congo and Eastern European countries like Lithuania and Romania.

- **Emigration and return migration:** Continuing emigration out of the country is marked by a change to new and more varied destinations, where emigrants are more likely to return home. This is referred to as 'return migration'. At the beginning of the century, Irish people were less likely than any other Europeans to return. This has now completely changed and return migrants are likely to be a force to be reckoned with in the coming years.

These changes in demographics obviously have an effect on employment and the learner's expectations regarding who they may be working with or for while they are on work experience. The workplace has become increasingly more multicultural, where learners can appreciate and identify with other work colleagues' nationalities and cultures.

## *Globalisation*

**Globalisation** means the impact that world events, world communications and world issues have on workplaces. In the twenty-first century, our reliance on international trade has both positive and negative effects.

- **Global communications:** The World Wide Web, e-mail, the internet, mobile phone technology and satellite communication have revolutionised world communication, allowing simple, quick access and exchange of global information, which can have both positive and negative effects on the workplace.

- **War and natural disasters:** Many products sold to the customer are imported, in particular oil, thus a change in world events, like the war in Iraq, can push up the price of oil and home heating oil in Ireland, causing the cost of living to rise. Natural disasters like tsunamis, hurricanes, landslides, earthquakes, etc. also affect people worldwide. For example, world oil prices increased substantially following Hurricane Katrina in 2005. Business transport costs were also severely affected with price increases in petrol and diesel.

- **Global economic changes:** If the US experiences a recession or economic downturn, Irish workers are also affected by a fall in demand for certain types of technological products made by US companies that are located here, resulting in unemployment.

- **Global changes in technology:** New technological goods available abroad and imported into Ireland can render some companies' goods obsolete. These companies then have to diversify in order to remain competitive and survive. For example, videos have been replaced by DVDs, etc.


## *Other factors affecting organisations and industries – PEST plus C*

What is PEST plus C?

- **P means political factors** like government decisions or local authority decisions, e.g. taxation decisions, government spending decisions.

- **E means economic factors** like a global economic downturn triggered by terrorism and a fall in the value of stocks and shares because of investors withdrawing their funds. This usually causes a fall in the value of a country's currency and can cause unemployment.

- **S means social factors,** describing social benefits or costs to a workplace. Examples of *social benefits* are car parking, bag packing and good customer service in retail outlets. Examples of *social costs* are pollution caused by a firm or an undesirable odour from a factory, e.g. a meat factory, all of which affect businesses and communities.

- **T means technological factors (rapid technological change),** where new technology speeds up the completion of tasks and may pose a risk to labour. Lack of up-to-date technology can be bad for productivity, and higher labour costs can result.

- **C means competition factors,** describing the negative or positive effects the location or existence of the nearest competitor can have on a business. For example, large chain stores locating near small specialised shops can cause the small shop to lose business. The larger outlet can avail of discounts and excellent credit terms (sometimes ninety days' credit) and pass these benefits on to the consumer in the form of lower prices. Examples of positive effects include hairdressers locating beside beauty salons where both may offer some similar services or products, but complement each other in many ways, thus helping both businesses.

# Review questions

The following questions can be used to identify and explain key issues influencing your chosen industry/area of work experience (or vocational area). Both positive and negative effects should be noted.

### 1. Which industry is your chosen workplace part of?

For example, a small shop in the local shopping centre is part of the retail industry, whereas an insurance company and a bank are part of the financial services industry.

## 2. Demographic changes.

Has this industry ever been affected by changes in population size or profile?

For example, the hotel and catering industry has had large numbers of non-nationals working in it due to the multicultural nature of the workforce in Ireland in recent years.

## 3. Globalisation and/or national or international economic issues.

Has this industry ever been affected by:

(a)  World economic changes, e.g. the US downturn/recession, the change to the euro, the boom in the Irish economy, changes in the housing market, etc.?

(b)  World and national events, e.g. foot and mouth disease, the war in Iraq, problems with terrorism, the rise in the price of oil?

(c)  Natural disasters, e.g. drought, earthquakes, hurricanes, landslides, flooding, etc.?

(d)  Global changes in technology?

## 4. Political issues.

Has this industry ever been affected by:

(a)  Changes in taxes?

(b)  The change to the euro?

(c)  Any other political decisions or lobby groups?

For example, vending machine suppliers had to alter their machines to suit the new euro currency, which would have proven very costly. The smoking ban has affected pubs and restaurants and created a need for outdoor rainproof spaces for smokers. Publicans have also had to buy patio heaters.

**5. Social issues.**

Has this industry ever been affected by:

(a)  Problems with pollution?

(b)  Availability of car parking beside the workplace?

(c)  Customer service and facilities?

(d)  Kerb appeal?

**6. Technological issues.**

Has this industry ever been affected by:

(a)  New technology brought into the workplace, thereby creating a need for retraining, etc.?

(b)  Lack of up-to-date technology?

**7. Competition issues.**

Has this industry ever been affected by its nearest competitor, or is there a niche market?

**8. Future plans for the industry.**

Do you know if there are any changes planned for the future that will directly or indirectly affect the industry?

# How learning from other subject areas may be relevant to work experience

While it is particularly important that you gain work experience in a workplace that is relevant to your chosen course area, it is also important to create links between subjects on your course of choice. Consider the following examples.

- **Communications** will provide training in personal and interpersonal skills and highlight the importance of these in the workplace. It also enables learners to gain telephone skills, skills regarding how to chair a meeting and negotiating skills. Students are also given an introduction to how meetings are regulated and summarised in the form of a set of narrative minutes. Advertising techniques and other types of visual communications can be linked to the main area of study. For example, learners may choose to use a piece of pottery (art students) or a play mat (child care students) that is their own creation to satisfy assessment requirements as well as understand the importance of subject links.

- **Customer service** will provide you with the skills necessary to deal courteously, effectively and efficiently with customers in the workplace.

- **Business administration** will teach you about organisational structures and will help you identify what type of structure your workplace fits into. It also explains the meaning of human resource management (HRM) or personnel and issues connected with staff welfare and staff care and conditions.

- **Information and communication systems (ICS)** identifies the importance of e-mail and the internet as well as computer hardware and software. Business health and safety awareness is also provided in the study of ergonomics, i.e. the need for workers to have adequate ventilation, heating, eye protection (computer visors) and upright seating while at work. It also helps you understand that regular breaks and intervals of body movement, especially leg movement, are important in order to prevent deep-vein thrombosis (DVT), a potentially fatal condition that is linked to computer and office jobs where workers must remain stationary, e.g. at a computer station or office desk.

The knowledge gained from additional modules as well as your chosen course therefore comes as a package, where most if not all modules feed into workplace learning in one form or another.

## STUDENT WORKBOOK QUESTIONS

### Exercise 6: Key Issues influencing trends in a workplace's industry

### Now go to your student workbook at the back of this book.

1. In the space provided on p. 130, state which industry your chosen workplace is part of, then indicate how the following key issues influence trends in the industry connected to your vocational area:

   • Demographic changes.
   • Globalisation and/ or national or international economic issues.
   • World and national events.
   • Natural disasters.
   • Political issues.
   • Social issues.
   • Technological issues.
   • Competition issues.
   • Changes planned for the future.

# Sample contract of employment

Dear _____,

We have a temporary vacancy in ................. and I have pleasure in offering you temporary employment in this post.

A Statement of your Terms and Conditions of Employment is enclosed. I should be grateful if you would signify your acceptance of the offer by signing the attached copy of this letter and returning it to ................. .

Your employment is temporary, commencing on Monday, 19 June and terminating on Friday, 28 July. The Unfair Dismissals Act 1993 shall not apply to a termination consisting only of the expiry of this term without its being renewed.

Please report for work to ................. at 9.00 a.m. on 19 June. You should bring with you your Income Tax Form P45. As you will see from the attached Terms and Conditions, your salary will be paid monthly, one month in arrears. This payment will be made on the second Friday of each month for any employment with us during the previous month – therefore, you may be with us six or seven weeks before you receive any payment. If this is likely to cause you difficulty, you should approach your assistant manager concerning the arrangement of advance payment of some of your salary.

If you are unable to start on that date, please contact me without delay. If you require further information or clarification on any aspect of this correspondence, please get in touch with me at ext. ............. .

I would like to take this opportunity to wish you every success and happiness during your period of temporary employment with us.

Yours sincerely,

I accept the temporary position as offered. I acknowledge receipt of a Statement of the General Terms and Conditions of my Employment and Staff Rules. I have read these and accept them as the terms and conditions of my contract of employment with ............. . I shall report for duty as requested.

SIGNED: _____ DATE: _____

# Sample statement of terms and conditions of employment

## 1. NATURE OF EMPLOYEMNT
You will be employed on a temporary basis.

## 2. SECRECY
You are required to treat all information gained as a result of your employment with ...... as strictly confidential, both during and after your employment with ...... . For this purpose you will be required to sign a Declaration of Secrecy Form.

## 3. WORKING HOURS
The normal working week is from Monday to Friday inclusive.
The normal working day may vary, but overtime is calculated on a daily basis in respect of each completed quarter-hour worked in excess of 7.25 hours (exclusive of one hour's lunch break).
Your normal starting and finishing times will be advised to you by your manager/head of department.
Payment for overtime work will be at such rates as are in force from time to time, and is based on completed quarter hours worked in excess of the normal day.
(Details of eligibility and current overtime rates are available from managers/heads of departments.)

## 4. SALARY
Your salary will be at the rate of €...... per week, payable monthly. In addition, overtime is payable at the current agreed rates, at present €...... per hour.

## 5. HOLIDAYS
Provided you have worked at least 120 hours in a calendar month, you will be entitled to holidays at the rate of one and three-quarters working days per month worked, this leave to be taken by agreement with your manager/head of department but before six months' continuous employment has elapsed.
If you have worked less than 120 hours in a calendar month, you will be entitled to six hours paid leave for every 100 hours worked and to proportionately less for periods of less than 100 hours worked, provided:

- you are normally expected to work at least eight hours each day.
- you have at least thirteen weeks' continuous service. These thirteen weeks are not included when calculating annual leave entitlements.

Holiday pay and payment in lieu of accrued holidays on termination of employment will be paid at the rate of €...... per day.
You will be entitled to the same bank/public holidays as permanent officials, details of which are available from your manager/head of department (if you have worked 120 hours in the five weeks preceding the holiday or have thirteen weeks' continuous employment and are normally expected to work more than eight hours a week).

## 6. BENEFITS NOT APPLYING TO THIS EMPLOYMENT

You will not have entitlement to benefits applicable to permanent employees, e.g. club subscriptions, pension benefits, staff loan facilities, etc.

## 7. SICK LEAVE

If you are unable to attend work because of illness, your manager/head of department should be notified as early as possible on the first day.

Where you have cumulative service of one year or more, you become entitled to paid certified sick leave up to a maximum of four weeks in any one year. However, there will be no pay for absence due to sick leave during the first year of employment. You may be required to see the company doctors or a doctor nominated by the company at any stage during your employment. You will be entitled to see any medical report made at the request of the company and said report shall not be used by ...... except for lawful purposes.

## 8. NOTICE OF TERMINATION OF EMPLOYMENT

The Minimum Notice and Terms of Employment Act 1994 will apply to notice of termination by ...... or by you or your employment. The statutory minimum notice which must be given is one week. ...... reserves the right to give payment in lieu of notice.

## 9. MATERNITY

The Maternity Protection of Employees Act 1994 shall apply to female temporary staff regarding maternity leave and the right to return to work. (Details available from Personnel Manager.)

## 10. GRIEVANCE AND DISCIPLINARY PROCEDURES

A listing of the principal staff rules is attached. Detailed Grievance and Disciplinary Procedures have been devised to ensure that fair and prompt arrangements exist for dealing with grievance or disciplinary matters. Grievance and Disciplinary Procedures will be provided on request.

## 11. ALTERATIONS IN TERMS AND CONDITIONS

Alterations in your Terms and Conditions of Employment will be advised, normally by general circular or memorandum to branches/departments, as they occur from time to time.

## 12. GENERAL

It is understood that you will perform, to the best of your ability, all duties assigned to you and will at all times obey all reasonable instructions given to you.

# Sample declaration of secrecy form

Dear Sir/Madam,

I acknowledge receipt of the letter informing me of my contract with ...... and I accept the temporary contract on the terms outlined in that letter.

In addition I hereby **SOLEMNLY AGREE, UNDERTAKE AND DECLARE**:

(1) I will keep secret and never use, attempt to use, divulge or attempt to divulge information to anyone or body concerning the affairs of ...... or any of its customers as may come to my knowledge or with which I may become acquainted while in the employment of ...... or in any other manner whatsoever, save to other officials of ...... whose province it is to know the same, or with the consent of ...... or by the authority of a court of law and I will not by word or deed say or do anything which may prejudice or injure ...... or be calculated to disclose the business or concerns thereof or of any customer of ...... . These restrictions shall apply during my employment with ...... and at any time thereafter.

(2) I will make known without delay to my general manager and the directors of ...... any fraud or irregularities on the part of any employee or customer of ...... or any other person tending to prejudice ...... which may come to my knowledge.

(3) During my period of employment with ...... I will not work for a competitor of ...... and any other work I am/become involved in will not interfere in any way with my capacity to carry out the duties ...... require of me.

(4) I will observe all rules and regulations of ......

DATE: _____

SIGNED: _____

WITNESS: _____

# Chapter 3

## Learner Record Part 2: Experience in the Workplace

You need to familiarise yourself with the organisation where you have gained work experience. You must document the background of the business, the staff structure as well as internal and external factors that affect the organisation.

You also need to outline the following:

- The work experience job title, e.g. office assistant, trainee hairdresser, trainee programmer, trainee travel agent.
- Place of work.
- Branch in country/world (if applicable).
- Section (if applicable), e.g. hotel restaurant, office or bar.
- Department (if applicable), e.g. sales or accounts department.
- Times of work.
- Name and title of superior(s).

## Workplace background

You should briefly describe:

- The nature of the business (service or product).
- Its history and date of establishment.
- If it relocated.
- Number of branches/sections/departments.

- Ownership structure (sole trader, partnership, private or public limited company, state or semi-state body).
- Number of employees (including male/female breakdown).
- Size of premises.

## Staff structure

You should draw one or more organisational charts showing the staff structure, emphasising clear lines of authority. The duties and responsibilities of each staff member mentioned in the chart should be described. The student examples below are taken from different vocational areas.

Visual display charts, like bar and pie charts, can be used to depict data that applies to small, medium and large organisations. The following pie chart represents the age and gender breakdown of a company's workforce.

**FIGURE 3.1: STAFF AGE PROFILE**

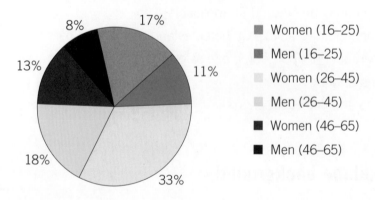

Total number employed: 147

## *Child care example*

### ORGANISATIONAL CHART OF A CRÈCHE

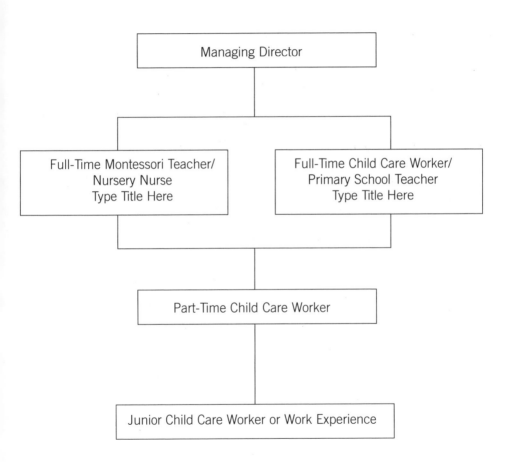

Managing Director

Full-Time Montessori Teacher/
Nursery Nurse
Type Title Here

Full-Time Child Care Worker/
Primary School Teacher
Type Title Here

Part-Time Child Care Worker

Junior Child Care Worker or Work Experience

## *Retail example*

### ORGANISATIONAL CHART OF A RETAIL OUTLET

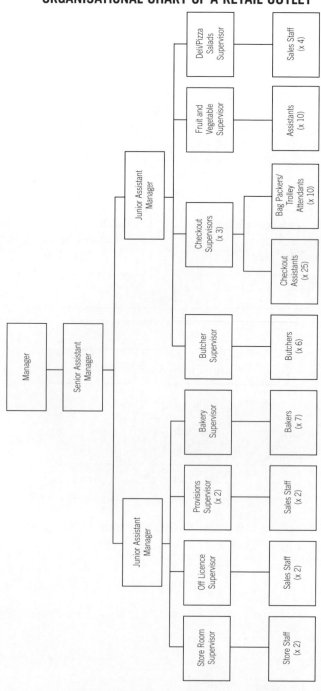

## Wholesale example

### ORGANISATIONAL CHART OF A WHOLESALER

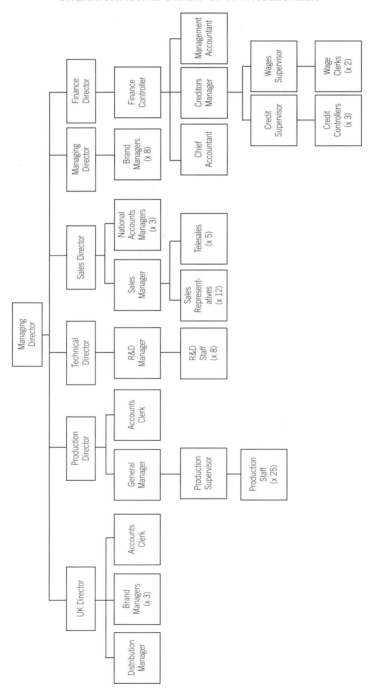

# Internal factors of the organisation

You should also explore the internal factors that apply to your work placement and be able to explain how these factors affect the organisation.

An organisation may be affected by a variety of internal factors that dictate whether or not it is efficiently run. You could use the following questions to identify and reflect on these factors:

• Is the management style effective?
• Is the staff suitably qualified and well motivated?
• Is there a sufficient number of staff available?
• Is there an air of co-operation between members of staff?
• Is there a feeling of belonging to a team?
• Is there a problem with ongoing demands for higher wages?
• Is the equipment modern and well serviced?

## Communications methods and professional ethics

Good, well-defined communications methods will make for an effective, efficient organisation where everyone is fully informed and understands the workings of the organisation.

There are five channels of communication that apply to every organisation. Information travels from:

• Manager to manager.
• Manager to staff.
• Staff to staff.
• Staff to customers, suppliers, the general public and anyone else outside the organisation.
• Manager to customers, suppliers, the general public and anyone else outside the organisation.

The following questions could be used to assess whether the organisation has good communication methods and whether good professional ethics are practised in the workplace:

- How do the staff and the management communicate, e.g. through meetings, noticeboards, staff web zones, intercom, internal memos, etc.?
- How do staff members communicate information to customers, e.g. advertising methods, word of mouth, etc.?
- How does the manager(s) take information into and send information out of the organisation, or are other sub-managers delegated to do this work?
- What policy is in place to ensure that professional ethics are adhered to? For example, is customer confidentiality always respected? Do staff members always act professionally when dealing with customers?

### Health, hygiene and safety in the workplace

The following questions could be used to assess whether the organisation adheres to health, hygiene and safety guidelines:

- Does the business have a health, hygiene and safety policy? Is there a safety officer/representative on the staff?
- How does the organisation implement the policy? For example, are there appropriate exit signs? Are fire drills and precautions in place to ensure the safety of employees and the public?
- Does the business have a safety statement?
- What kind of insurance does the business have to insure itself against public liability? Are there any other types of insurance in place?
- Is there training for staff in the areas such as fire prevention and first aid?
- Are there anti-bullying or anti-racist policies in place as part of the health and safety policy? What steps do the managers take to implement these?

# External factors of the organisation

An organisation may be affected by a variety of external factors that dictate whether or not it is efficiently run. Use the following questions to identify and reflect on these factors.

- Who are the organisation's competitors?
- What kinds of market forces affect the demand, supply and prices of the goods produced or the services offered by the organisation?
- Are deliveries of supplies (incoming raw materials) or products (outgoing deliveries) often late? If so, how are sales affected?
- Have interest rate fluctuations affected the organisation in the past?
- Do currency fluctuations (exporters, importers, tourism, etc.) affect the organisation in any way, e.g. the change to the euro?
- How do rising global industrial or occupational wage demands affect the organisation?

In the case of service-type organisations, the following external factors might be identified:

- Changing birth and death rates (demographics) in a region can affect a service, e.g. demand for nursing homes or child care facilities.
- Natural disasters, e.g. earthquakes, floods, volcanoes, etc., would affect travel agents and tour operator services.
- The growth in e-commerce (buying and selling on the internet) could adversely affect those organisations not promoting their product or service on the World Wide Web.

Explore the external factors that apply to your work placement and be able to explain how these factors affect the organisation.

## STUDENT WORKBOOK QUESTIONS

### Exercise 7: Workplace Details

**Now go to your student workbook at the back of this book.**

1. Give a brief account of the history, size, ownership and product/service profile of your workplace.
2. Draw the organisational chart of your workplace in the space provided on p. 135, with clear lines of authority and clear chart headings.

3. Describe the duties of the staff that are outlined in your organisational chart.

4. List the communication methods that were used in the workplace.

5. List the professional ethics that were practised by staff and managers.

6. Explain what health, safety and hygiene policy was implemented in the organisation.

7. Explain the external factors that affect your workplace.

# Work experience diary

You should compile a detailed description of the work you undertook while on work experience.

Day-to-day experiences, both positive and negative, should be outlined. New knowledge gained and evidence of the ability to learn from negative as well as positive experiences and challenges should be shown in this report. The learner report should be based on the work experience diary located on p. 157.

The work experience diary should give a detailed explanation of:

- The variety of work tasks carried out while on work experience.
- How work was handled.
- Personal challenges encountered.
- Work-related challenges encountered.
- Existing skills improved upon.
- New practical or interpersonal skills learned.

# Examples of work tasks

## TABLE 3.1

| | |
|---|---|
| **Catering** | Food costing.<br>Vegetable preparation.<br>Soup making.<br>Baking.<br>Stir-fry techniques. |
| **Fashion design** | Embroidery.<br>Printed textiles.<br>Advertising.<br>Fashion buying.<br>Graphic skills. |
| **Multimedia production** | Digital movie processing.<br>Authoring web design.<br>Image processing.<br>Animation. |
| **Child care** | Games supervision.<br>Montessori supervision.<br>Food preparation.<br>Feeding babies.<br>Changing babies. |

# Experience gained

You need to reflect on the practical, personal and interpersonal experiences gained by undertaking various tasks.

Remember:

- **Practical skills** are physical work tasks, e.g. learning to use office equipment, table service duties, colouring and perming hair, graphic design techniques, etc.
- **Personal skills** include getting to work on time, meeting deadlines, etc.
- **Interpersonal skills** are people skills, e.g. dealing courteously with the employer or supervisor, customers, service users or clients and people you work with.

The following examples explain how the tasks you are given are categorised as practical, personal and interpersonal skills.

## Media/broadcasting student

Maeve MacDonagh, a media/broadcasting student on work experience at Live 75 FM, learned the following skills.

*Practical skills:*

- She learned to shoot footage and edit it using Avid Xpress and Adobe Premere Pro.
- She learned how to do vox-pops and edit them using Adobe Audition/Cool Edit.

*Personal skills:*

- Maeve learned how to be more patient when organising shoots.
- She learned to work well as part of a team.

## Computer student

Mary Ryan is on work experience in Compumarket Ltd. As part of an advertising procedure, her supervisor requested her to directly mail a variety of catalogues to potential customers. In completing this task, the experience would have taught her the following skills.

*Practical skills:*

- She learned how to sift through customer records from a database file in order to shortlist appropriate prospective customers.
- She gained experience using the Mail Merge facility in Microsoft Word.

*Personal skills:*

- She learned how to work on her own initiative.
- She learned how to be more adaptable and flexible.

*Interpersonal skills:*

- Mary learned how to carry out supervisor instructions efficiently.
- She learned how to work efficiently with colleagues to complete the task.

## Tourism student

Colm Downey, on work experience at Going Places Travel Agency, must deal with a client from the enquiry through to the booking stage. In completing this task, the experience would have taught Colm the following skills.

*Practical skills:*

- How to use the computerised Galileo system efficiently. Colm was able to obtain booking information and confidently book a holiday for the client.
- He learned administration skills, including writing a receipt after the client pays (by cheque, credit card or cash) and forwarding the receipt to the client.

*Personal and interpersonal skills:*

- To be more punctual and improve on attendance.
- To be more competent in dealing with awkward customers.

## Hairdressing student

Siobhán McMahon, on work experience at Wedge Styles salon, learned the following skills.

*Practical skills:*

- To wash, set and blow-dry hair.
- To apply a semi-permanent colour and a conditioning treatment.

*Personal and interpersonal skills:*

- To acquire a high level of tolerance working in a busy environment.
- To work effectively as part of a multi-skilled team.

## Child care student

Eileen Daly, on work experience at Little Treasures Crèche, learned the following skills.

*Practical skills:*

- To quickly and efficiently change babies' nappies, paying attention to hygiene.
- To assist in toilet training toddlers in co-operation with parents.
- To assist in introductory Montessori instruction.

*Personal skills:*

- To co-ordinate a range of children's activities, simultaneously maintaining a good degree of control.
- To strictly adhere to the time routine of the crèche for different activities, e.g. meal times, nappy changing and break times, etc.

*Interpersonal skills:*

- To delicately and efficiently give full comprehensive information to parents regarding their child's or children's progress using the report book for parents.

## Art and design student

Séamus Brophy, on work experience at Graphic Design Studios, learned the following skills.

*Practical skills:*

- To produce a book cover from designs using Quark Xpress.
- To layer photographs using Adobe Photoshop.

*Personal and interpersonal skills:*

- To work on his own initiative.
- To contribute his own design ideas to a group discussion.

# Challenges encountered

You may encounter personal and work-related challenges while on work experience.

*Personal challenges:*

- Getting to work – good attendance.
- Getting to work on time – punctuality.
- Completing work tasks – ability to do the work.
- Completing tasks on time – meeting deadlines.

*Work-related challenges:*

- Dealing with awkward customers, service users or clients.
- Dealing with unco-operative colleagues.
- Dealing with a difficult employer/superior.

## *Personal challenges*

- Have you become more punctual? Has your attendance improved?
- Are you more being more accurate and precise in the execution of work tasks?
- Do you get tasks completed on time?
- Do you organise your work tasks in a diary in order of priority?
- Do you attend to work tasks immediately or do you still postpone them?

## *Work-related challenges*

*Awkward customers or clients:*

- Did you learn to listen and take note of the problem?
- Did you apologise for the inconvenience (even though you were not at fault) and maintain a high degree of professional courtesy?
- Did you investigate options to remedy the problem?
- Did you offer to compensate the customer or client?
- Was the problem resolved in a manner satisfactory to the customer or client?

*Difficult colleagues:*

- Have you learned to avoid open confrontation with colleagues?
- Do you realise the importance of not backbiting colleagues?
- Did you maintain courtesy towards colleagues at all times?
- Did you articulate your viewpoints to colleagues in a coherent and fair manner?
- Do you realise the importance of looking at the wider picture when it comes to a breakdown of relations between colleagues?

*Difficult employer/superior:*

- Did you learn to accept constructive criticism with dignity?
- Did you articulate your viewpoints to your employer/superior in a calm and coherent manner?
- Have you learned how to work well with a difficult employer/superior?

# Learner checklist

## TABLE 3.2

| Headings | Suggested layout of contents | Tick (✓) | Teacher comment |
|---|---|---|---|
| Report introduction | List your name, award title and code, course title and definition and name of workplace. | | |
| Work description and skills gained/ improved on | List personal, interpersonal, practical or technical skills gained or improved on. | | |
| Challenges | List the personal and work-related challenges you encountered during work experience. | | |
| Positive learning from challenges | List the positive things that you learned from both the negative and positive experiences. | | |
| Conclusion | Highlight new learning that has taken place. | | |

## STUDENT WORKBOOK QUESTIONS

### Exercise 8: Workplace Description and Skills gained while on Work Experience

### Now go to your student workbook at the back of this book.

**Use your work experience diary as a guide to writing this summary (see p. 157).**

1. What day(s) did you gain work experience, and what were your times of work?

2. What tasks did you carry out while on work experience, and how did you handle them? Describe in detail the work you undertook while on work experience.

3. Did you encounter any personal or work-related challenges? If so, how did you handle them?

4. Did you improve on any skill that you already have? (Break down your answer into personal, interpersonal, practical or technical skills; see Chapter 2.)

5. Did you learn any new skills? (Break down your answer into personal, interpersonal, practical or technical skills; see Chapter 2.)

# Chapter 4

## Learner Record Part 3: Work Experience Review and Evaluation

The purpose of review and evaluation is to critically analyse learning goals achieved, skills gained or improved upon and experiences and challenges encountered. You are encouraged to evaluate how you would now manage a similar work experience situation – what could have been done differently?

**Note:** This report should be linked with your planning and preparation (see Chapter 2).

## Analysis and reflection on experiences

**Self-assessment:**

- Did you experience frustration in the workplace?

**Goals achieved and skills learned:**

- Did you achieve your learning goals?
- Have you gained the skills you hoped to gain (practical, personal, interpersonal and technical skills)?

**Personal challenges:**

- What positive personal experiences did you learn from?
- What negative personal experiences did you learn from?

**Work-related challenges:**

- What positive work-related experiences did you learn from?
- What negative work-related experiences did you learn from?

**What would you have done differently?**

- Would you have chosen a different workplace, or perhaps researched the organisation in greater detail?
- Would you now remember to think before you speak and to go with the flow?
- Would you express your opinion more openly next time?
- Would you organise your personal life differently to suit your work situation?
- Would you approach customers, managers, colleagues, etc. differently?
- If you have leadership skills, do you now realise that you may disagree more than you agree with your colleagues, and in the future will avoid confrontation, realising that you have to learn to do things your manager/superior's way?

# Your future

Since the Celtic Tiger boom, Ireland has much to offer job seekers (see Chapter 1). There are now many choices of jobs and careers available in Ireland today.

You need to have a definite idea of your future career plans and be able to answer the question 'Where do you see yourself in five years' time?'

You should also be able to explain the significance of your current studies and the usefulness of the qualification that you will receive. This should include possible links to further or higher education or future plans to do short courses.

You should always be willing to improve your qualifications. For example, a student who did a management course at night after starting with a one-year certificate course in business and computers eventually got his degree. Or a student who started off with an introductory course in nursing studies realised that physiotherapy is what she wanted to do.

# STUDENT WORKBOOK QUESTIONS

## Exercise 9: Analysis and Reflection on Experiences

## Now go to your student workbook at the back of this book.

1. What would you have done differently if you were starting work experience again?

2. Were the learning goals that you set before starting work experience realistic? (See Exercise 3, Chapter 2.)

3. Did you learn new skills or improve on skills you already had? Were these the 'target skills' that you listed in your plan? (See Exercise 2, Chapter 2.)

4. Were the challenges you encountered the ones you expected to experience? Could you have handled these situations differently? Indicate whether they were personal or work-related challenges and whether they were positive or negative.

5. What are your future career plans in light of having gained this work experience?

6. How has the work experience helped you to gain a fuller understanding of the importance of the subjects you are studying as part of your course?

7. What further education and training will your qualifications allow you to avail of?

8. Has this work experience improved you personally, e.g. are you now more confident, punctual, etc.?

9. Has this work experience improved your work skills, e.g. greater attention to detail, meeting deadlines, etc.?

10. In what ways did this work experience match your expectations?

# Chapter 5

## Skills Demonstration

## The supervisor's report

The supervisor's report forms an important part of the overall assessment of the work experience participant's FETAC Work Experience module. It is a record of assessment of a broad range of vocational, practical and interpersonal communication skills demonstrated by the work experience participant while in the workplace.

Areas that the supervisor must assess are:

- Interest in the work.
- Awareness of health and safety practices.
- Appropriate dress.
- Ability to follow instructions.
- Quality of agreed/assigned work.
- Practical skills.
- Use of workplace equipment.
- Punctuality.
- Attendance at workplace.
- Relating to co-workers.
- Relating to supervisor.
- Communicating with customers.
- Acceptance of direction/criticism.
- Initiative.
- Adaptability.

The following blank report form, reproduced from the FETAC Work Experience module, is given to the supervisor.

# Sample supervisor's report

## Supervisor's report
### Work Experience (W20008)

| | |
|---|---|
| Participant's Name | Centre/School Name ____ Tel No ____ |
| Organisation/Company Name | Supervisor's Name ____ No of days worked ____ |

**Guidelines** This report forms an important part of the overall assessment of work experience for certification.
It should be completed by a supervisor/manager who has observed the participant in the workplace.
Please indicate the participant's performance by placing a tick for each of the criteria under one of the headings. *Excellent should only be used in cases of outstanding performance.*

| Criteria | Excellent | Very Good | Good | Satisfactory | Unsatisfactory | Unable to Assess |
|---|---|---|---|---|---|---|
| Interest in the work | | | | | | |
| Awareness of health & safety practices | | | | | | |
| Appropriate dress | | | | | | |
| Ability to follow instructions | | | | | | |
| Quality of agreed/assigned work | | | | | | |
| Practical Skills | | | | | | |
| Use of workplace equipment | | | | | | |
| Punctuality | | | | | | |
| Attendance at workplace | | | | | | |
| Relating to co-workers | | | | | | |
| Relating to supervisor | | | | | | |
| Communicating with customers | | | | | | |
| Acceptance of direction/criticism | | | | | | |
| Initiative | | | | | | |
| Adaptability | | | | | | |

**Further Comments**

Brief description of work undertaken by candidate

Any comments or suggestions on work experience arrangements

Any other comments.

Signature of Workplace supervisor ____ Date ____

Issued by National Council for Vocational Awards

# Guidelines for the supervisor

It is important that the supervisor completes the form as accurately and as objectively as possible in order to give a measured indication of the participant's abilities and application. In completing the form, the supervisor gives a brief description of the work carried out by the participant and is encouraged to comment on what he/she believes are more suitable arrangements for work experience to be conducted, based on the particular vocational area their organisation is connected to.

The supervisor should maintain regular contact with the course provider to ensure best-quality learner work for the good of both the organisation and the work experience participant. This interaction will lead to enhanced learner performance in the workplace. It is also a positive way of addressing any skills shortages that may be apparent.

Thirty per cent of the entire marks for the FETAC Work Experience module are set aside for the marking of the supervisor's report form. In grading the form, the examiner awards marks based on the supervisor's entries, as follows:

- Satisfactory in at least ten categories: fifteen to twenty marks.
- Good in all categories or very good in at least ten categories: twenty-one to twenty-three marks.
- Very good in all categories or excellent in at least ten categories: twenty-four to thirty marks.

**Note:**

1. In the work practice mode where the teacher/tutor/co-ordinator elects to monitor and assess the learner, the teacher/tutor completes the report form.

2. This report does not apply to APEAL learners (see Chapter 7), as they will already have attained accreditation for current or prior experience of work in a vocational area directly related to the qualification being sought.

# Guidelines for the learner

While on work experience, you must be aware that you are being assessed in the following areas.

### Interest in the work.

A lack of enthusiasm and a general lackadaisical attitude to work becomes apparent to a supervisor very quickly. An eagerness to undertake and carry out work with a positive, cheerful disposition is what is required.

### Awareness of health and safety practices.

It is mandatory that you make yourself aware of the heath and safety procedures within the organisation. A quiet conversation with the supervisor on this topic before embarking on work experience is recommended.

### Appropriate dress.

While some organisations may enforce a strict dress code, most nowadays accept neat, casual dress in the workplace. Runners, dirty and/or torn jeans are not recommended. Heavy make-up and the application of too much scent are generally frowned upon. A little common sense is required when dressing for the workplace.

### Ability to follow instructions.

Listening is an essential part of communication. If you are given a set of instructions at the start of the day, it is good practice to make note of each one in the order that they were given. If you get an instruction that you do not understand, always ask for clarification before embarking on the task. By simply repeating a question, the learner can gain the required clarification from the supervisor.

**Quality of agreed/assigned work**.

Poorly carried out or incomplete work does not reflect well on you. If you get a sense that the supervisor is unhappy with the work, always ask for guidance on how the work could have been carried out better.


**Practical skills**.

In learning a skill, two steps are required:

* The observation of the skill being carried out by an expert practitioner.
* The frequent repetition of the skill by the learner to fully master it.

Whether observing a hair stylist applying a hair colour or a computer technician installing a hard disk, the ease with which the expert carries out the skill should be noted.


**Use of workplace equipment**.

The prudent use and care of workplace equipment is important. For example, a painter does not leave his paintbrushes strewn on the floor at the end of the day, a network engineer does not use work time to download music albums for her iPod or a forklift operator does not stack pallets too high.


**Punctuality**.

Consistent late arrival for work is frowned upon in most organisations. If you are going to be late for work for an unforeseen reason, call the supervisor and give an indication of when you will arrive.


**Attendance at workplace**.

Inconsistent attendance at work leads to dismissal in most organisations. If you are unfit to attend work, call the supervisor and indicate the reason for your absence.

**Relating to co-workers**.

After the initial introductory period, most workers settle in as part of an effective work team. An ability to work alongside colleagues to complete tasks is essential in most organisations.

**Relating to supervisor**.

While on work experience, you must listen carefully to the supervisor's instructions and carry them out to the best of your ability.

**Communicating with customers**.

The common saying that 'the customer is always right' is a good motto to adopt when dealing with members of the general public. Without the customer, the business will quickly fail. You can occasionally be confronted with difficult customers who wish to 'vent their spleen'. In such situations, remain calm and do not engage in an argument. Call the supervisor if you feel that you may not be able to deal with the customer's queries or complaints.

**Acceptance of direction/criticism**.

You can expect some constructive direction/criticism from the supervisor, given to help you become a more effective worker. Do not develop a defensive approach to the supervisor's guidance. Listen carefully and be prepared to ask further questions to clarify the points being made to you.

**Initiative**.

Initiative is described as 'the power or ability to begin or to follow through energetically with a plan or task without prompting or direction from others.' It implies enterprise and determination. It is a positive attribute, but the new worker must be careful not to undertake a radical course of action without first discussing the idea with the supervisor.

**Adaptability**.

The ability to adjust your approach and be flexible in changing and challenging situations is another quality that is very useful in the workplace.

## STUDENT WORKBOOK QUESTIONS

### Exercise 10: Skills Demonstration

**Now go to your student workbook at the back of this book.**

1. Write a brief account of the main points that are noted on the supervisor's form that you should pay attention to while on work experience.

2. Note particular areas of assessment that you need to keep a watch on while on work experience.

# Chapter 6

## Industry Analysis

## Analysis of the workplace employment sector of choice

While you are on work experience, you need to find out what industry your workplace is part of. In the context of your workplace, you are required to profile this as part of an industry assignment. Consider the examples in the table below.

### TABLE 6.1

| Which industry is your workplace part of? | Is the workplace a member of or does it have connections with industry organisations? | What is the staff union representative body or the employer representative association? |
|---|---|---|
| Media | Broadcasting Complaints Commission (BCC), The Broadcasting Commission of Ireland (BCI) | National Union of Journalists (NUJ) |
| Construction | The Construction Federation Industry of Ireland | Services, Industry, Professional and Technical Union (SIPTU) |
| Insurance | The Insurance Institute or Institute of Bankers | Irish Bank Workers Union |
| Retail | RGDATA or Retail Ireland | SIPTU |
| Child care | The National Childcare Association | SIPTU |

| Small and medium enterprises (SMEs) | IBEC SFA | SIPTU |
|---|---|---|
| Art and cultural industry | The Arts Council | Duchas |
| Communications | An Post | Communications Workers Union (CWU) |
| Transport | Iarnród Éireann Bus Éireann | National Bus and Rail Workers Union, SIPTU or Amalgamated Transport and General Workers Union (ATGWU) |

Other industry information is available from:

- Industrial Development Authority: www.idaireland.com.
- Enterprise Ireland: www.enterpriseireland.ie.
- Irish Congress of Trade Unions: www.ictu.ie.

# The nature of the work

What is the precise nature of the work being carried out? Can the work be categorised as either manufacturing or service oriented? For example, a kitchen company that makes and supplies kitchens is connected with manufacturing, whereas a service industry might be a hair stylist or travel agent because a service is being provided.

# Location

Where is the premises located? Is it freehold or leasehold? The nature of the work can determine the location of the premises. A coffee shop is usually in a location with much passing trade, e.g. a town's main street, while a company specialising in car alarm installations may be best located in a business park. Is the business suited to a rural or urban location? An example of a rural business location might be a wind energy farm, while an urban business could be a taxi business.

# Industry change and global issues

Has the industry or general requirements within the industry changed due to EU membership and the conversion to the euro? Has there been any controversial issues surrounding the industry, either nationally, internationally or globally? Some examples are:

- The foot and mouth disease, affecting the agriculture and tourism industries.
- Health and safety concerns regarding phone masts, affecting the communication industry.
- 9/11 terrorism, affecting the airline and tourism industries.
- The US economic slowdown, affecting the computer industry.
- The cessation of the Shannon Airport transatlantic stopover, affecting the tourism industry, or the introduction of new airline routes.

# Numbers engaged in the industry

You should learn the numbers of people employed in the industry. This is often available from government websites like Forfás (www.forfas.ie) or the Economic and Social Research Institute (ESRI, www.esri.ie). The Organisation for Economic Cooperation and Development (OECD, www.oecd.org) and www.answers.com are also useful websites to source industry information.

# Range of occupations within the industry

The range of occupations within the business should be ascertained. For example, the construction industry has a wide and varied range of associated occupations, e.g. architects, block layers, carpenters, electricians, plasterers, plumbers and steel fixers, whereas the number of occupations in primary teaching is limited, e.g. head teacher, class teacher and classroom assistant.

# Organisational chart

An organisational chart is an excellent way of obtaining an overview of an industry workforce. The various areas within the industry become apparent and chains of command can be easily identified from an organisational chart, starting at the top of the pyramid, which usually notes the government minister in charge of the industry area, and perhaps national and international branches. An industry profile in this format might also note very senior managing directors and chairpersons, e.g. Tony Ryan and Michael O'Leary, chief executives in Ryanair.

# Potential for growth

Is the work area within the industry being analysed contracting or expanding? Are you aware of any decision by the management to take on more workers, or alternatively to downsize the current workforce? For example, rationalisation in the banking sector and the consequent decrease in the number of bank branches is leading to a decrease in the number of banking personnel required, while the rapid growth of wireless technologies is leading to an increase in the number employed selling, deploying and supporting these new technologies, e.g. communications companies like Vodafone and $O_2$.

# Employment and career opportunities in the sector

Before training for a particular career, a good starting point is to research the employment opportunities and associated salary scales in that area. You can research this field in a number of ways.

- **Interview people employed in the area:** Examples of questions that can be asked are:

  (a) What are the employment prospects in the area?

  (b) Is the area contracting or expanding?

  (c) If you were starting again, would you have chosen this career? Why or why not?

  (d) What path did you take to your current position?

  (e) How long have you held your current position?

  (f) Do you plan to spend the remainder of your working life in this occupation?

- **Examine employment agency job listings:** These details can be obtained by either dropping into an agency or visiting their website.
- **Monitor newspaper job advertisements:** This old-fashioned way of looking for work can give an indication as to employment trends in various sectors.
- **Visit the relevant bodies' websites:** Most employment areas have governing bodies overseeing standards and changes within that area. Examples of employment sectors and relevant websites are shown in Table 6.2.

**TABLE 6.2**

| Industry | Websites |
|---|---|
| Media | Media Live: www.medialive.ie<br>The Broadcasting Commission of Ireland: www.bci.ie<br>The Broadcasting Complaints Commission: www.bcc.ie |
| Accountancy | Institute of Chartered Accountants in Ireland: www.icai.ie |
| Banking | Allied Irish Banks: www.aib.ie<br>Bank of Ireland: www.boi.ie |
| Beauty | Confederation of International Beauty Therapy and Cosmetology: www.cibtac.com |
| Child care | National Childcare Information Center: www.nccic.org (US) |
| Hairdressing | National Hairdressers' Federation: www.nhfuk.com (UK) |
| Fashion | Irish fashion: www.fashion.ie |
| Information technology | Irish Computer Society: www.ics.ie |
| Retail | Retail, Grocery, Dairy and Allied Trades' Association (RGDATA): www.rgdata.ie |
| Sports therapy | The Society of Sports Therapists: www.society-of-sports-therapists.org (US) |
| Tourism | Irish Tourist Board: www.ireland.ie<br>Tourism Ireland: www.tourismireland.com |

**TABLE 6.3**

| SIMI | The Official Voice of the Motor Industry (www.simi.ie) |
|---|---|
| FSAI | The official website providing information for the food industry, e.g. deli, hotel and catering and restaurant businesses (www.fsai.ie) |
| FilmNet | Assists and promotes the TV and film industry in Ireland, offering a one-stop shop of film information, including production facilities, actors, locations, technicians, etc. (www.filmnet.ie) |

# Occupation analysis

You must analyse one occupation from the employment sector of your choice. It is essential that the following sections are covered in this analysis.

## *Job specification*

Select a position in your work experience placement and interview the person who holds the job. You could compile a questionnaire in order to analyse this job area. Questions regarding qualifications and experience necessary to gain such a job could be included in this questionnaire.

A sample questionnaire might include questions such as the following.

- What is your formal job title?
- What are your duties and areas of responsibility?
- What qualifications do you think would be necessary to gain a similar position to yours?
- Would it be useful to study other courses, and which ones would you recommend?
- How many years' experience do you think would be necessary to gain a similar position to yours?
- Would it be useful to gain a variety of related work experiences, and what types would you recommend?

The following headings could then be used to bring the information together.

### Job title

What is the title of the chosen occupation, e.g. banker, hairdresser, software developer?

## Education and training required

What precise educational qualifications and/or training are required to do the job? For example, a person wishing to embark on a career in primary teaching would require a Bachelor of Education degree to gain employment.

## Experience required

If the person has experience in carrying out a particular task, it is reasonable to expect that the task will be completed satisfactorily and within a set time. In most cases, a person who has never performed the task before will carry it out less efficiently. The old saying that 'there is no substitute for experience' is very true. A crèche manager will have spent a considerable length of time working with children, while a head gardener will have spent many years working with many varieties of flowers and shrubs.

A person working as an apprentice was often said to be 'serving his/her time', i.e. gaining necessary experience from working with older, more experienced workers in a variety of work situations. A young electrician can gain a wealth of experience from a master when working together to totally rewire a number of different types of houses and outbuildings.

The numbers of years' experience required to become competent should be noted.

## *Positive and negative aspects*

In embarking on any career, there will be positive and negative aspects. If a particular career is for you, then the positives will far outweigh the negatives. The following set of questions should be asked when analysing a particular occupation.

- Is the length of time required to train for this occupation excessively long?
- Can I make a satisfactory living in this occupation?

- Does this occupation suit a particular personality?
- What aptitudes are preferable for a career in this area?
- How long does it normally take to rise to the top of the profession/trade?
- Can I move to a different county or country and still be employable in the same occupation?
- Do I have any relatives working in this area?
- Will my job consist of a good deal of travelling?
- Will I have to work as part of a team?
- Are there associated benefits, e.g. long holidays, voluntary health contributions?
- Can I serve my time and then branch out as a sole trader?
- Are the work hours unsociable, e.g. restaurant chef?
- Does the job require constant retraining, e.g. IT personnel?

## Employment opportunities in the organisation

Examine the different occupations in your work placement and identify future areas of opportunity where job prospects might arise, e.g. retirement, promotions or future expansion.

- Does the business plan to extend its premises in the near future?
- Does the business intend to recruit more staff?
- Does the business plan to expand its range of products or services?
- Does the business plan to relocate?
- Would it be in your interest to study a particular course with a view to gaining a job with the organisation?

## STUDENT WORKBOOK QUESTIONS

**Exercise 11: Analysis of Workplace Employment Sector of Choice**

**Now go to your student workbook at the back of this book.**

1. What industry is your workplace part of? Does it have a representative body?

2. Is the staff or are the managers represented by any particular organisation?

3. Discuss the nature of the work in the workplace, e.g. whether it is product or service oriented, freehold or leasehold, etc. Explore the range of occupations in the industry.

4. Explain the following factors: (a) the location of the workplace (b) whether it has been affected by industry change or diversification (c) if and why numbers in the industry have increased or decreased.

5. Indicate whether the workplace has been affected by expansion or contraction of operations within the industry.

6. Explore any controversial issues surrounding the industry.

7. Draw an industry organisational chart in the space provided on p. 154, with the government minister in charge of the industry at the top of the hierarchy.

8. Select an occupation within the workplace or industry and document both the occupation and the qualifications needed to apply for such a position in detail.

9. What areas of work will the qualification you expect to gain allow you to work in?

# Chapter 7

## Work-Based Learning (APEAL)

The work-based learning mode is designed to enable learners to gain accreditation for current or prior experience of work in a vocational area directly related to the certificate being sought.

The process used to assess prior work-based learning is Accreditation of Prior Experience, Achievement and Learning (APEAL). It applies, for example, to those learners who would be re-entering the education system after a number of years. Many are mature students participating in either the Back to Education (BTE) or the Vocational Education Opportunities Schemes (VTOS). Their entitlement to be assessed in this way depends on their employment track record. If a BTE or VTOS student has access to information on their previous workplace where they participated in work that is connected with their vocational area of study, they do not need to look for work experience and can gain accreditation through APEAL.

## Portfolio of assessment

A learner wishing to gain accreditation through the APEAL mode must submit a portfolio of assessment, including the learner record and assignment.

# The learner record

This includes:

- A job description that details the activities undertaken in work.
- A record of work, including a completed CV and a workplace reference.
- A review and evaluation of the learner's time in the workplace, to include:
  - A critical reflection on personal and vocational experience.
  - A discussion of the challenges encountered, both personal and work related.
  - A discussion of the positive aspects, both personal and work related.
  - A discussion of learning, both personal and work related.
  - An outline of future plans in light of workplace experiences.

The learner record may be presented in a variety of media, including written, oral, graphic, audio and visual or any combination of these. Before undertaking a compilation of material for the learner record, see Chapters 2, 3 and 4.

# The assignment

The course co-ordinator devises a brief that requires the learner to investigate their vocational award area. The completed submission should include:

- A description of the industry/sector and its range of occupations.
- An analysis of the qualifications and experiences needed for work associated with one occupation in the vocational area.
- A discussion on the employment and career opportunities in the vocational award area.

Before undertaking the assignment, see Chapter 6.

The following is a list of useful websites on work-based learning and work experience.

- **Career directions**: www.careerdirections.ie.
- **Finding work experience**: www.ssv.uce.ac.uk/WorkExperience/experience-students-finding.htm.
- **The importance of work experience**: www.e-skills.com/Careers-Site/Routes-into-Work/Work-Experience/431.
- **Structured workplace learning**: www.sofweb.vic.edu.au/voced/structured_workplace_learning/.
- **Turning age to your advantage:** www.le.ac.uk/careers/matureadvantage.html.
- **Volunteering for work experience**: www.nald.ca/fulltext/heritage/ComPartnE/ExprncE.htm.
- **Work-based learning:** www.learningthroughwork.co.uk/work_based_learning.
- **Work experience**: www.work-experience.org.
- **Work placements**: www.bbc.co.uk/radio1/onelife/work/options/work_exp.shtml.
- **Work placement advice**: www.hcima.org.uk/content/jobs_placements/documents/jobs_placement_advice_students.html.

# Student Workbook:
## Work Experience Portfolio

## EXERCISE 1: PERSONAL INTRODUCTION

1. Write an introduction to your student workbook by introducing yourself.
   Give a very brief description of your course, subjects being studied,
   proposed work experience details and any other personal details.

Name: _____

College: _____

Class: _____

Course and qualification: _____

Dates of work experience: _____

Contact number: _____

Name of organisation: _____

Supervisor's name and contact details: _____

Number of days/hours of experience: _____

Position held in organisation: _____

2. What I know about work and work experience in the twenty-first century and my future career plans.

_____

_____

_____

_____

_____

_____

_____

_____

_____

3. Display a critical awareness of how the nature of work and work practices have changed in recent years.

_____

_____

_____

_____

_____

_____

_____

_____

_____

4. Explain how necessary you think it is to obtain work experience.

_____

_____

_____

_____

_____

_____

_____

_____

_____

_____

_____

_____

_____

_____

_____

# EXERCISE 2: SKILLS AUDIT

1. My personal skills audit (see Chapter 2). (Note: Apply your analysis to your chosen area of study and work.)

| Skills I have | Excellent | Very good | Good | Fair | Poor |
|---|---|---|---|---|---|
| | | | | | |
| | | | | | |
| | | | | | |
| | | | | | |
| | | | | | |
| | | | | | |
| | | | | | |
| | | | | | |
| | | | | | |
| | | | | | |
| | | | | | |
| | | | | | |
| | | | | | |
| | | | | | |
| | | | | | |

* Course providers, supervisors, tutors or teachers of different vocational areas could select and provide the learner with an appropriate set of skills for inclusion on this sheet.

2. Now be more specific and list your personal, interpersonal, practical and technical skills (see Chapter 2 for a definition of these skills), stating how you hope to learn or improve on them from this work experience and where you originally learned them.

| Skills I hope to learn or improve on from this work experience | How I hope to learn or improve on these skills | Where I originally learned these skills |
|---|---|---|
| *Personal skills* | | |
| 1. _____ | _____ | _____ |
| 2. _____ | _____ | _____ |
| 3. _____ | _____ | _____ |
| 4. _____ | _____ | _____ |
| 5. _____ | _____ | _____ |
| *Interpersonal skills* | | |
| 1. _____ | _____ | _____ |
| 2. _____ | _____ | _____ |
| 3. _____ | _____ | _____ |
| 4. _____ | _____ | _____ |
| 5. _____ | _____ | _____ |
| *Practical skills* | | |
| 1. _____ | _____ | _____ |
| 2. _____ | _____ | _____ |
| 3. _____ | _____ | _____ |
| 4. _____ | _____ | _____ |
| 5. _____ | _____ | _____ |

| Skills I hope to learn or improve on from this work experience | How I hope to learn or improve on these skills | Where I originally learned these skills |
|---|---|---|
| *Technical skills* | | |
| 1. _____ | _____ | _____ |
| 2. _____ | _____ | _____ |
| 3. _____ | _____ | _____ |
| 4. _____ | _____ | _____ |
| 5. _____ | _____ | _____ |

3. State how these skills would prove to be an asset to the organisation that you are applying to for work experience.

_____

_____

_____

_____

_____

_____

_____

_____

_____

_____

_____

## SUMMARY CHECKLIST

You must remember to check that you include the following in your student workbook.

| Exercises 1 and 2 | Completed |
|---|---|
| 1. Introduce myself and briefly explain who I am and what I know about work and work experience in the twenty-first century. | |
| 2. Identify and rate my general skills. | |
| 3. Identify my existing skills more specifically, including those that I hope to improve on, indicating where I originally learned them (personal, interpersonal, practical and technical skills). | |
| 4. Explain how these skills would prove to be an asset to my workplace. | |

# EXERCISE 3: GOALS FOR WORK EXPERIENCE

1. Now set and list your goals for work experience and what skills you hope to learn (see Chapter 2 for an explanation and examples of learning goals).

    (a) My goals for work experience:

    _____

    _____

    _____

    (b) New **personal skills** I hope to learn from this work experience:

    _____

    _____

    _____

    (c) New **interpersonal skills** I hope to learn from this work experience:

    _____

    _____

    _____

    (d) New **practical skills** I hope to learn from this work experience:

    _____

    _____

    _____

    (e) New **technical skills** I hope to learn from this work experience:

    _____

    _____

    _____

## *SUMMARY CHECKLIST*

You must remember to check that you include the following in your student workbook.

| Exercise 3 | Completed |
|---|---|
| 1. Identify my goals for work experience. | |
| 2. Identify new skills I hope to learn while on work experience. | |

# EXERCISE 4: CURRICULUM VITAE, LETTERS, INSURANCE FORMS, CONTRACTS OF EMPLOYMENT, JOB-FINDING SKILLS AND INTERVIEW PREPARATION

1. Create a rough draft of your CV (no longer than two pages), using the headings below to help you (see Chapter 2 for sample CV and layout instructions).

## CURRICULUM VITAE

| PERSONAL DETAILS | |
|---|---|
| EDUCATIONAL DETAILS | |

| SKILLS PROFILE | |
| --- | --- |
| **WORK EXPERIENCE** | |
| **REFEREES** | |

2. Create a rough draft of your letter of application for work experience (no longer than one page, spaced and paragraphed appropriately) (see Chapter 2 for sample and explanations of terms).

Inside name and address

Date

Salutation, i.e. Dear Sir/Madam

SUBJECT HEADING (blocked and bolded)

Body of letter – no more than three paragraphs

Complimentary close

Signature

_____

Line under handwritten name

Name typed with first letter capitals only

Enc. (if CV is attached)

3. In your portfolio of work, include any insurance letters, contracts or correspondences that you sent to or received from your prospective employer for work experience.

## *JOB-FINDING SKILLS*

**(See Chapter 2)**

4. How I plan to gain work experience using my job-finding skills:

_____

_____

_____

_____

_____

_____

_____

_____

_____

_____

5. (a) Preparations I made for the interview for work experience, including how I plan to dress, sit and speak and an analysis of my CV:

_____

_____

_____

_____

_____

_____

_____

_____

_____

_____

(b)  Why I am the best candidate for the position:

_____

_____

_____

_____

_____

_____

_____

_____

_____

_____

## *SUMMARY CHECKLIST*

You must remember to check that you include the following in your student workbook.

| Exercise 4 | Completed |
|---|---|
| 1. Write a rough draft of my CV details. | |
| 2. Draft a letter of application for work experience. | |
| 3. Include a letter of introduction to the employer (tutor letter) in my portfolio, as well as insurance letters or any other contracts or relevant documents received. | |
| 4. Explain how I plan to find work experience, listing my job-finding skills. | |
| 5. Explain how I prepared for the interview for work experience. | |

# EXERCISE 5: EMPLOYMENT EQUALITY, HEALTH AND SAFETY AND LEGISLATION

1. What I know about employment equality and the two main legal Acts underpinning it:

_____

_____

_____

_____

_____

_____

_____

_____

_____

2. An employer's main obligations are:

_____

_____

_____

_____

_____

_____

_____

_____

3. An employer can take positive action to prevent workplace discrimination by:

_____

_____

_____

_____

_____

_____

_____

_____

4. Ten pieces of current legislation relating to employment in Ireland are:

_____

_____

_____

_____

_____

_____

_____

_____

## SUMMARY CHECKLIST

You must remember to check that you include the following in your student workbook.

| Exercise 5 | Completed |
|---|---|
| 1. Indicate what I know about employment equality and the linked legal Acts. | |
| 2. List the employer's main obligations. | |
| 3. Explain how an employer can take positive action to prevent workplace discrimination. | |
| 4. Briefly list and explain ten pieces of current employment legislation. | |

## EXERCISE 6: KEY ISSUES INFLUENCING TRENDS IN A WORKPLACE'S INDUSTRY

1. (a)  Which industry is your chosen workplace part of?

    _____

    _____

    _____

   (b)  Has your industry been affected by *demographic changes*, e.g. changes in population size or profile?

    _____

    _____

    _____

    _____

    _____

    _____

   (c)  Has your industry been affected by *globalisation and/or national or international economic issues*, e.g. the US economy's downturn, the change to the euro, the boom in the Irish economy, changes in the housing market, etc.?

    _____

    _____

    _____

    _____

    _____

    _____

(d) Has your industry been affected by *world and national events*, e.g. foot and mouth disease, the Iraq War, problems with terrorism, the rise in the price of oil, etc.?

_____

_____

_____

_____

_____

_____

(e) Has your industry been affected by *natural disasters*, e.g. drought, earthquakes, hurricanes, landslides, flooding, etc.?

_____

_____

_____

_____

_____

_____

(f) Has your industry been affected by *political issues*, e.g. changes in taxes, the change to the euro, political decisions or lobby groups?

_____

_____

_____

_____

_____

_____

(g) Has your industry been affected by *social issues*, e.g. problems with pollution, availability of car parking beside the workplace, customer service and facilities, kerb appeal, etc.?

_____

_____

_____

_____

_____

_____

(h) Has your industry been affected by *technological issues*, e.g. lack of up-to-date technology, new technology brought into the workplace, etc.?

_____

_____

_____

_____

_____

_____

(i) Has your industry been affected by *competition issues*, e.g. affected by its nearest competitor or is there a niche market?

_____

_____

_____

_____

_____

_____

(j)  Are there any *changes planned for the future* that will directly or indirectly affect your planned workplace's industry?

_____

_____

_____

_____

_____

_____

2.  Briefly explain how knowledge gained from other subjects (modules) on your course may be relevant to your work experience:

_____

_____

_____

_____

_____

_____

_____

_____

_____

_____

## SUMMARY CHECKLIST

You must remember to check that you include the following in your student workbook.

| Exercise 6 | Completed |
|---|---|
| 1. Identify what industry your workplace is part of, then briefly indicate how key issues like demographic trends, globalisation and new technology have or may affect the industry that your workplace is part of. | |
| 2. Briefly explain how other subjects on your course are relevant to work experience. | |

# EXERCISE 7: WORKPLACE DETAILS

1. Give a brief account of the history, size, ownership and product/service profile of your workplace.

_____

_____

_____

_____

_____

_____

_____

_____

_____

2. Draw the organisational chart of your workplace in the space provided below, with clear lines of authority and clear chart headings (see Chapter 3 for sample charts).

3. Describe the duties of the staff outlined in the organisational chart of the workplace, from the top of the chart to the bottom (hierarchy).

_____

_____

_____

_____

_____

_____

_____

_____

_____

4. List the communication methods that were used in the workplace.

_____

_____

_____

_____

_____

_____

_____

_____

_____

5. List the professional ethics that were practised by staff and managers.

_____

_____

_____

_____

_____

_____

_____

_____

6. Explain what health, safety and hygiene policy was implemented in the organisation:

_____

_____

_____

_____

_____

_____

_____

_____

_____

7. Explain the external factors that affect your workplace.

_____

_____

_____

_____

_____

_____

_____

_____

_____

# EXERCISE 8: WORKPLACE DESCRIPTION & SKILLS GAINED WHILE ON WORK EXPERIENCE

1. What day(s) did you gain work experience, and what were your times of work?

_____

_____

_____

_____

_____

_____

_____

2. What tasks did you carry out while on work experience, and how did you handle them? Describe in detail the work you undertook while on work experience.

_____

_____

_____

_____

_____

_____

_____

3. Did you encounter any personal or work-related challenges? If so, how did you handle them?

_____

_____

_____

_____

_____

_____

_____

_____

4. Did you improve on any skill that you already have? (Break down your answer into personal, interpersonal, practical or technical skills; see Chapter 2.)

_____

_____

_____

_____

_____

_____

_____

_____

5. Did you learn any new skills? (Break down your answer into personal, interpersonal, practical or technical skills; see Chapter 2.)

_____

_____

_____

_____

_____

_____

_____

_____

_____

## *SUMMARY CHECKLIST*

You must remember to check that you include the following in your student workbook.

| Exercises 7 and 8 | Completed |
|---|---|
| 1. Explain the history, size, ownership and product/ service profile of your workplace. | |
| 2. Draw the organisational chart of your workplace. | |
| 3. Describe the duties of the staff outlined in the organisational chart of the workplace. | |
| 4. Describe what communications methods and what professional ethics were used in the workplace. | |
| 5. Explain how the health, safety and hygiene policy was implemented in the workplace. | |
| 6. List any external factors that affect your workplace. | |
| 7. State what day(s) you gained work experience and your times of work. | |
| 8. Describe the tasks you carried out while on work experience and how you handled them. | |
| 9. List any personal or work-related challenges you encountered and how you handled them. | |
| 10. State whether you improved on any skill that you already have. | |
| 11. State whether you learned any new skills. | |

# EXERCISE 9: ANALYSIS AND REFLECTION ON EXPERIENCES

1. What would you have done differently if you were starting work experience again?

_____

_____

_____

_____

_____

_____

_____

_____

2. Were the learning goals that you set before starting work experience realistic? (See Exercise 3, Chapter 2.)

_____

_____

_____

_____

_____

_____

_____

_____

3. Did you learn new skills or improve on skills you already had? Were these the 'target skills' that you listed in your plan? (See Exercise 2, Chapter 2.)

_____

_____

_____

_____

_____

_____

_____

_____

_____

_____

4. Were the challenges you encountered the ones you expected to experience? Could you have handled these situations differently? Indicate whether they were personal or work-related challenges and whether they were positive or negative.

_____

_____

_____

_____

_____

_____

_____

_____

_____

5. What are your future career plans in light of having gained this work experience?

_____

_____

_____

_____

_____

_____

_____

_____

_____

_____

6. How has the work experience helped you to gain a fuller understanding of the importance of the subjects you are studying as part of your course?

_____

_____

_____

_____

_____

_____

_____

_____

_____

7. What further education and training will your qualifications allow you to avail of?

_____

_____

_____

_____

_____

_____

_____

_____

_____

8. Has this work experience improved you personally, e.g. are you now more confident, punctual, etc.?

_____

_____

_____

_____

_____

_____

_____

_____

9. Has this work experience improved your work skills, e.g. greater attention to detail, meeting deadlines, etc.?

_____

_____

_____

_____

_____

_____

_____

10.In what ways did this work experience match your expectations?

_____

_____

_____

_____

_____

_____

_____

## SUMMARY CHECKLIST

You must remember to check that you include the following in your student workbook.

| Exercise 9 | Completed |
|---|---|
| 1. Indicate what you would have done differently. | |
| 2. Indicate whether your learning goals were realistic. | |
| 3. Document whether your target skills that you hoped to learn or improve on were realistic and achieved. | |
| 4. State whether the challenges you encountered were the ones you expected to experience and if you could have handled these situations differently. | |
| 5. Describe your future career plans in light of this work experience. | |
| 6. State how this work experience has allowed you to fully understand the importance of the subjects you are studying. | |
| 7. State the further education and training available to you. | |
| 8. Indicate how this work experience has improved you personally. | |
| 9. Indicate how this work experience has improved your work skills. | |
| 10. State if this work experience matched your expectations. | |

# EXERCISE 10: SKILLS DEMONSTRATION

1. Write a brief account of the main points that are noted on the supervisor's form that you should pay attention to while on work experience.

_____

_____

_____

_____

_____

_____

_____

_____

_____

2. Note particular areas of assessment that you need to keep a watch on while on work experience.

_____

_____

_____

_____

_____

_____

_____

_____

_____

## SUMMARY CHECKLIST

You must remember to check that you include the following in your student workbook.

| Exercise 10 | Completed |
|---|---|
| 1. A brief account of the main things that are noted on the supervisor's form that you should pay attention to while on work experience. | |
| 2. Particular areas of assessment that you need to keep a watch on while on work experience. | |

# EXERCISE 11: ANALYSIS OF WORKPLACE EMPLOYMENT SECTOR OF CHOICE

1. What industry is your workplace part of? Does it have a representative body?

_____

_____

_____

2. Is the staff or are the managers represented by any particular organisation?

_____

_____

_____

_____

_____

_____

_____

_____

_____

_____

3. Discuss the nature of the work in the workplace, e.g. whether it is product or service oriented, freehold or leasehold, etc. Explore the range of occupations in the industry.

_____

_____

_____

_____

_____

_____

_____

_____

_____

_____

4. Explain the following factors: (a) the location of the workplace (b) whether it has been affected by industry change or diversification (c) if and why numbers in the industry have increased or decreased.

_____

_____

_____

_____

_____

_____

_____

_____

_____

5. Indicate whether the workplace has been affected by expansion or contraction of operations within the industry.

_____

_____

_____

_____

_____

_____

_____

_____

6. Explore any controversial issues surrounding the industry.

_____

_____

_____

_____

_____

_____

_____

_____

_____

7. Draw an industry organisational chart in the space provided, with the government minister in charge of the industry at the top of the hierarchy.

8. Select an occupation within the workplace or industry and document both the occupation and the qualifications needed to apply for such a position in detail.

9. What areas of work will the qualification you expect to gain allow you to
   work in?

   _____

   _____

   _____

   _____

   _____

   _____

   _____

   _____

   _____

   _____

## SUMMARY CHECKLIST

You must remember to check that you include the following in your student workbook.

| Exercise 11 | Completed |
|---|---|
| 1. State what industry your workplace is part of and if it has a representative body. | |
| 2. State whether the staff or managers are represented by any particular organisation. | |
| 3. Discuss the nature of the work in the workplace, and explore the range of occupations in the industry. | |
| 4. Explain the following factors: (a) the location of the workplace (b) whether it has been affected by industry change or diversification (c) if and why numbers in the industry have increased or decreased. | |
| 5. Indicate whether the workplace has been affected by expansion or contraction of operations within the industry. | |
| 6. Explore any controversial issues surrounding the industry. | |
| 7. Draw an industry organisational chart, with the government minister in charge of the industry at the top of the hierarchy. | |
| 8. Select an occupation within the workplace or industry and document both the occupation and the qualifications needed to apply for such a position in detail. | |
| 9. List the areas of work the qualification you expect to gain will allow you to work in. | |

# Work Experience Diary

## Work Experience Diary: Day 1

Name: _____  Work experience day(s): _____

Class: _____  Date(s): _____

**Work undertaken (list tasks):** _____

**Existing skills improved upon:**

1. Practical skills      _____

2. Personal skills       _____

3. Interpersonal skills  _____

**New skills learned:**

1. Practical skills      _____

2. Personal skills       _____

3. Interpersonal skills  _____

**How work was handled:**  _____

_____

_____

**Challenges encountered:**

1. Personal challenges     _____

2. Work-related challenges _____

**Other comments:**  _____

_____

_____

# Work Experience Diary: Day 2

Name: _____     Work experience day(s): _____

Class: _____     Date(s): _____

**Work undertaken (list tasks):** _____

**Existing skills improved upon:**

1. Practical skills          _____

2. Personal skills          _____

3. Interpersonal skills     _____

**New skills learned:**

1. Practical skills          _____

2. Personal skills          _____

3. Interpersonal skills     _____

**How work was handled:**     _____

_____

_____

**Challenges encountered:**

1. Personal challenges       _____

2. Work-related challenges   _____

**Other comments:**          _____

_____

_____

# Work Experience Diary: Day 3

Name: _____    Work experience day(s): _____

Class: _____    Date(s): _____

**Work undertaken (list tasks):** _____

**Existing skills improved upon:**

1. Practical skills          _____

2. Personal skills          _____

3. Interpersonal skills     _____

**New skills learned:**

1. Practical skills          _____

2. Personal skills          _____

3. Interpersonal skills     _____

**How work was handled:**     _____

_____

_____

**Challenges encountered:**

1. Personal challenges       _____

2. Work-related challenges   _____

**Other comments:**          _____

_____

_____

# Work Experience Diary: Day 4

Name: _____ Work experience day(s): _____

Class: _____ Date(s): _____

**Work undertaken (list tasks):** _____

**Existing skills improved upon:**

1. Practical skills _____

2. Personal skills _____

3. Interpersonal skills _____

**New skills learned:**

1. Practical skills _____

2. Personal skills _____

3. Interpersonal skills _____

**How work was handled:** _____

_____

_____

**Challenges encountered:**

1. Personal challenges _____

2. Work-related challenges _____

**Other comments:** _____

_____

_____

# Work Experience Diary: Day 5

Name: _____  Work experience day(s): _____

Class: _____  Date(s): _____

**Work undertaken (list tasks):** _____

**Existing skills improved upon:**

1. Practical skills  _____
2. Personal skills  _____
3. Interpersonal skills  _____

**New skills learned:**

1. Practical skills  _____
2. Personal skills  _____
3. Interpersonal skills  _____

**How work was handled:**  _____
_____
_____

**Challenges encountered:**

1. Personal challenges  _____
2. Work-related challenges  _____

**Other comments:**  _____
_____
_____

# Work Experience Diary: Day 6

Name: _____ Work experience day(s): _____

Class: _____ Date(s): _____

**Work undertaken (list tasks):** _____

**Existing skills improved upon:**

1. Practical skills _____

2. Personal skills _____

3. Interpersonal skills _____

**New skills learned:**

1. Practical skills _____

2. Personal skills _____

3. Interpersonal skills _____

**How work was handled:** _____

_____

_____

**Challenges encountered:**

1. Personal challenges _____

2. Work-related challenges _____

**Other comments:** _____

_____

_____

# Work Experience Diary: Day 7

Name: _____ Work experience day(s): _____

Class: _____ Date(s): _____

**Work undertaken (list tasks):** _____

**Existing skills improved upon:**

1. Practical skills      _____

2. Personal skills      _____

3. Interpersonal skills    _____

**New skills learned:**

1. Practical skills      _____

2. Personal skills      _____

3. Interpersonal skills    _____

**How work was handled:** _____

_____

_____

**Challenges encountered:**

1. Personal challenges    _____

2. Work-related challenges   _____

**Other comments:** _____

_____

_____

# Work Experience Diary: Day 8

Name: _____  Work experience day(s): _____

Class: _____  Date(s): _____

**Work undertaken (list tasks):** _____

**Existing skills improved upon:**

1. Practical skills _____

2. Personal skills _____

3. Interpersonal skills _____

**New skills learned:**

1. Practical skills _____

2. Personal skills _____

3. Interpersonal skills _____

**How work was handled:** _____

_____

_____

**Challenges encountered:**

1. Personal challenges _____

2. Work-related challenges _____

**Other comments:** _____

_____

_____

# Work Experience Diary: Day 9

Name: _____ Work experience day(s): _____

Class: _____ Date(s): _____

**Work undertaken (list tasks):** _____

**Existing skills improved upon:**

1. Practical skills          _____

2. Personal skills          _____

3. Interpersonal skills     _____

**New skills learned:**

1. Practical skills          _____

2. Personal skills          _____

3. Interpersonal skills     _____

**How work was handled:**    _____

_____

_____

**Challenges encountered:**

1. Personal challenges       _____

2. Work-related challenges   _____

**Other comments:**          _____

_____

_____

# Work Experience Diary: Day 10

Name: _____ Work experience day(s): _____

Class: _____ Date(s): _____

**Work undertaken (list tasks):** _____

**Existing skills improved upon:**

1. Practical skills _____

2. Personal skills _____

3. Interpersonal skills _____

**New skills learned:**

1. Practical skills _____

2. Personal skills _____

3. Interpersonal skills _____

**How work was handled:** _____

_____

_____

**Challenges encountered:**

1. Personal challenges _____

2. Work-related challenges _____

**Other comments:** _____

_____

_____

# Work Experience Diary: Day 11

Name: _____ Work experience day(s): _____

Class: _____ Date(s): _____

**Work undertaken (list tasks):** _____

**Existing skills improved upon:**

1. Practical skills _____

2. Personal skills _____

3. Interpersonal skills _____

**New skills learned:**

1. Practical skills _____

2. Personal skills _____

3. Interpersonal skills _____

**How work was handled:** _____

_____

_____

**Challenges encountered:**

1. Personal challenges _____

2. Work-related challenges _____

**Other comments:** _____

_____

_____

# Work Experience Diary: Day 12

Name: _____     Work experience day(s): _____

Class: _____     Date(s): _____

---

**Work undertaken (list tasks):** _____

**Existing skills improved upon:**

1. Practical skills          _____

2. Personal skills           _____

3. Interpersonal skills      _____

**New skills learned:**

1. Practical skills          _____

2. Personal skills           _____

3. Interpersonal skills      _____

**How work was handled:**    _____

_____

_____

**Challenges encountered:**

1. Personal challenges       _____

2. Work-related challenges   _____

**Other comments:**          _____

_____

_____

# Work Experience Diary: Day 13

Name: _____ Work experience day(s): _____

Class: _____ Date(s): _____

**Work undertaken (list tasks):** _____

**Existing skills improved upon:**

1. Practical skills _____

2. Personal skills _____

3. Interpersonal skills _____

**New skills learned:**

1. Practical skills _____

2. Personal skills _____

3. Interpersonal skills _____

**How work was handled:** _____

_____

_____

**Challenges encountered:**

1. Personal challenges _____

2. Work-related challenges _____

**Other comments:** _____

_____

_____

# Work Experience Diary: Day 14

Name: _____     Work experience day(s): _____

Class: _____     Date(s): _____

---

**Work undertaken (list tasks):** _____

**Existing skills improved upon:**

1. Practical skills        _____

2. Personal skills        _____

3. Interpersonal skills    _____

**New skills learned:**

1. Practical skills        _____

2. Personal skills        _____

3. Interpersonal skills    _____

**How work was handled:**    _____

_____

_____

**Challenges encountered:**

1. Personal challenges     _____

2. Work-related challenges _____

**Other comments:**        _____

_____

_____

# Work Experience Diary: Day 15

Name: _____ Work experience day(s): _____

Class: _____ Date(s): _____

**Work undertaken (list tasks):** _____

**Existing skills improved upon:**

1. Practical skills          _____

2. Personal skills          _____

3. Interpersonal skills     _____

**New skills learned:**

1. Practical skills          _____

2. Personal skills          _____

3. Interpersonal skills     _____

**How work was handled:**    _____

_____

_____

**Challenges encountered:**

1. Personal challenges       _____

2. Work-related challenges   _____

**Other comments:**          _____

_____

_____